Teaching
Green

Others books by Damian Randle:

Peace and War (Edward Arnold, 1984)
Population and Food (Edward Arnold, 1986)
Various educational resources in Alternative Technology

Teaching Green

A parent's guide
to education
for life on Earth

DAMIAN RANDLE

GREEN
PRINT

First published in 1989 by
Green Print
an imprint of The Merlin Press Ltd
10 Malden Road, London NW5 3HR

ISBN 1 85425 011 6

1 2 3 4 5 6 7 8 9 10 :: 99 98 97 96 95 94 93 92 91 90 89

Phototypeset by Input Typesetting Ltd, London

Printed in England by Biddles Ltd., Guildford
on recycled paper

Acknowledgements

This book could not have been written without the help, direct and indirect, of two groups of people. They are the *Green Teacher* people: co-operative members, contributors and subscribers; and the 'Quarry' people: my colleagues at the Centre for Alternative Technology. My work on *Green Teacher* arose out of my work at the Centre, and neither this book nor anything else would have been possible for me without the stimulus and support that I have been lucky enough to receive from these two halves of my life.

I have been particularly assisted by a number of publications: the *Times Educational Supplement*'s 'Governors' Guide', which is still available, inexpensively, from the *T.E.S.*; the historical writing of Harold Silver and John Lawson; the first few issues of *Holistic Education Review*, the excellent new journal edited by Ron Miller in Massachusetts; the publications associated with the Human Scale Education Movement, especially those of Philip Toogood and Roland Meighan; and – most inspirationally – the output of the Centre for Global Education at York University. Details of all these are in the Resources section at the end of the book.

I am thankful beyond words for the patience and kindness of Cynthia Ferguson and Sabrina Wise, wordprocessors extraordinaires!

But the one person absolutely crucial to the whole enterprise has been Joan Randle, my wife and co-worker: what remains of my personal sanity is thanks to her. Whatever is good about the book is ultimately due to the uncountable instances of her aid and encouragement which keep the *Green Teacher* and Teaching Green shows on the road.

Whatever is not so good about the book – the mistakes and the omissions – is my responsibility. Please do join in the dialogue I ask for, so that we can put them right!

Damian Randle
June 1989

Contents

Introduction

'Now then children: Are you sitting comfortably? Then I'll begin.

'Our story begins back in the 1990s. You remember the historical investigations of that period which we completed last term? You discovered how the poisoning and the destruction of the environment began to stop, and the habit of some people acting like greedy monsters and bullying the poorer, weaker ones, began to stop. And how human beings began treating each other as whole people, with respect for each other's bodies and feelings and spiritual truths, and how we began treating all the rest of life in our ecosystem — the earth — as sacred?

'And what happened to the mega-machine — that system of gobbling up the earth, and swallowing up people, and mashing everything up so that a few people could profit? How did it happen that people realised how they had been treated and decided to change things, change themselves, change the way we looked after each other and the earth? Yes, of course you know: parents and teachers began co-operating properly in the education of their children, and it was what everyone had known in their bones was needed: green education. Education for a green future.

'And soon after that, children began to stand up and demand more and more respect and responsibility and before long they — and *their* children — had begun to save life on earth. They worked together to dismantle the mega-machine.

'How did it all start? I'm not sure, but my grandmother told me of a book. When she was a girl, an old headmaster — they had those things then — showed it to her. "Green Teacher", or "Teaching Green", or something like that it was called. Anyway,

1

that was only the start. Many, many people worked very, very hard, over the generations since then, before we could say we — and life on earth — were safe.'

That teacher in the year 2089 (or 2189) is, of course, wrong to ascribe such importance to one publication. But things are beginning to happen. We're all greening now, aren't we? When a ruthless right-wing British Prime Minister, the President of the USSR, and the Pope all agree on something, something is afoot. It will be up to our children to make sure that the powers that got us into this mega-machine mess are not the ones whose ideas we follow in clearing it up.

Neither will that teacher, I am sure, wish to imply that the sort of changes required — involving enormous shifts of economic and political power — will have happened entirely through the personal transformation of individuals. Such transformations — via personal change in adults, and/or education of whatever form — do sometimes seem to carry the entire hopes of some sections of the green movement. But no-one who understands the mega-machine and its history, and the history of its radical opponents, can ignore the need for collective action. The state is in the hands of the mega-machine, and that must change.

At another level, such advances, in education and other areas, as we have managed in the last century or so have been achieved by collective action. The greening of radical politics is overdue: traditional labourism is bankrupt. But if we try to separate green politics from the best of the radical tradition, that teacher will not be saying those things in 2089, or ever.

People who start to think about green matters usually begin at the shallow level — cleaner rivers, protect the ozone layer. Then, if they go on thinking, they go much deeper: what ways of *thinking*, what ways of *being*, have led us to mistreat the earth and abuse each other? So we start to question, and to change, our paradigms — the assumptions that we make, which colour the information we receive and dictate how we deal with new ideas.

The old paradigm on which our culture is based – man has conquered nature; man can exploit the earth and, for ever, gain more and more material goods; man can exploit other men, and all women; man can treat himself and other people as mechanical components, or economic units, whose purpose is to serve the mega-machine – has been obviously faulty for a long time. A new paradigm, with co-operation and sensitivity to the earth and to each other as the dominant value, is required.

This is what people usually mean when they talk about moving in the green direction. The deeper people go into it, the more a sense of wholeness, a desire for holism, becomes important. When we know how all the elements of the ecosystem are linked together, we cannot, as happens today, then mistreat one part and hope that others are unaffected. When we learn to treat people, including ourselves, as whole beings — physically, emotionally, spiritually — we cannot then deal with another person as if with a machine for consuming. Nor do we want to tolerate a hospital treating us as lumps of flesh, or a school treating our children as vessels into which to pour knowledge and skills.

Teaching green, then, could be called holistic education, and that is a good description.

Can we have it? Yes. When? That depends on how well we work together. This book, if it works, will help parents to decide what sorts of things they want for their children's green education, and to have the confidence to co-operate with teachers and others in moving in that direction.

In order to do this we will need, first, to have a look at the education system as it is today (a brief administrative introduction: Chapter 1). Then, more importantly, we need to ask: 'How have the inspiring ideas in education developed? Where did they come from? Are they still around today?' (Chapter 2). Then we will look at how we came to have the system we have today (a brief historical introduction: Chapter 3).

Next, having at least an idea of where we are and how we got here, we need to ask the crucial question: 'What do we want? Where do we want to go?' (Chapter 4).

So then we ask, 'Is green teaching, of the sort we want to build on, going on in schools and colleges?' 'Are people writing interesting material today which points the way for tomorrow?' In other words, 'Are there any beacons in what can seem very much like the darkness?' Part Two gives a selection.

Finally, there is a checklist that parents and teachers may find useful in their local school or college or local education authority, and a resource list which will enable readers to go a lot further on their own.

The most important period in the struggle for the greening of education will be that critical time when there are enough people, with enough good ideas and enough enthusiasm, to form the critical mass that makes success inevitable. That could be a long time away, but possibly sooner than we think. As editor of *Green Teacher* magazine, I have been pleasantly surprised by the number of teachers and students who, despite the narrowness and shallowness of attitudes in the past — or, of course, because of this — are determined to teach green.

Very often each individual feels s/he is alone, and many of the letters I receive are full of the joy teachers feel on learning that there are many others with similar ideals.

Relative to the aims of the system as a whole, organised for the benefit of the mega-machine, these teachers — and local authority advisers in numbers which may surprise you — are subversives. They can only benefit from the creative support and co-operation of parents. Let us all work together as joyful subversives, to replace teaching for the mega-machine with teaching, and learning, green.

I hope this book helps.

PART ONE
THE SYSTEM
AND HOW TO CHANGE IT

CHAPTER ONE
Education in Britain: administration and national curriculum

In order to be able to work on, or in, the system, we will need an outline of what it looks like and how it works. I'm afraid I do not know of a way of making it not boring, so I suggest that, to enjoy this chapter, you do the following.

Invite a friend into your home and indulge yourselves with a large dose of a recreational chemical, preferably coffee. Then put on silly hats and have ready a supply of balloons and those gadgets that shoot out and make alarming sounds when blown. Then read the important bits twice. The first time, do so quietly and diligently, as (I assume) you would have done back in your days as a conscientious school-student, because you may be tested, in most un-green fashion, later. The second time (this is called reinforcement) you do so aloud, together or alternately, doing as many different funny voices as possible, and doing whatever takes your fancy with the balloons, gadgets, etc.

Now for the serious bit. . .

The basic administrative unit of educational provision in England and Wales is the Local Education Authority (LEA). This, in effect, is the education committee of the Local Authority — County Council, Metropolitan Borough Council, London Borough. The LEA builds and runs schools, employs teachers, provides money (some from government, some from

---

I am indebted for much of the information here to the *Times Educational Supplement*'s 'The Governors' Guide', a wonderful resource for all parents who wish to understand the system. The *TES* address is given in 'Resources'.

rates) for buying equipment and books, and employs advisers/inspectors to help with curriculum development and to check up on progress.

Curriculum

On curriculum, i.e. what and how the children learn, there was until recently a lot of freedom. LEAs were free, and schools within LEAs were free (to a greater or lesser degree depending on where you were) and teachers within schools were free (to a greater or lesser degree depending which school you were looking at) to interpret their job in the way they saw fit, according to local needs, resources and skills. This has changed with the new, centrally imposed, national curriculum, which, under the 1988 Education Act, schools must follow. This curriculum is to be broad and balanced, and to promote the spiritual, moral, cultural, mental and physical development of pupils at the school and of society.

The national curriculum covers pupils aged 5 to 16, and is made up of three 'core subjects' — English, maths and science — and seven 'foundation subjects' — history, geography, technology, art, music, physical education, and in secondary schools a modern language. It will take up about 70 per cent of the school day. Schools also have a legal obligation to teach religious education.

The Secretary of State can lay down programmes of study for all subjects of the national curriculum, revise the curriculum and programmes when necessary, set attainment targets, and make arrangements for assessment. Teachers and schools will decide what materials and, insofar as they are left free to do so, what teaching methods to use to implement the national curriculum.

The national curriculum applies to all maintained schools, including grant-maintained schools. It began to be introduced in primary and secondary schools in September 1989. It does not apply to city technology colleges or private schools. Schools can apply to the Secretary of State to be exempted from the national curriculum to engage in new curriculum development.

Under the national curriculum, each child should do work in the following 'areas of experience': the aesthetic area (music, art, drama, design); the human and social area (how people live, how society changes); language and literature; mathematics; the moral area (practical moral learning, reasoning, personal and social education); the spiritual area (religious education); the physical area (physical education, dance, games); and the scientific and technological areas.

School Management

On the subject of management of the school, the 1988 Act has devolved a lot of responsibility from the LEA to the school — effectively to the head and governors.

The 1988 Act gives all secondary schools and primary schools with more than 200 pupils control of their own spending. All LEAs are required to send the DES proposals for dividing money between these schools. LEAs also have the option of allowing smaller primary schools to manage their resources.

The formula for calculating how the money is actually dealt with is fairly simple, but there are so many possible exemptions and variations that each case will be different. The LEA *must* take certain items, like inservice training costs, out of the money it doles out, and it *may* also take out other items, like provision for special needs. These discretionary items must not total more than 10 per cent of the total schools budget. The money left is distributed: 75 per cent according to the numbers, ages and stages of pupils (14-year-olds get more than 9-year-olds, etc.); 25 per cent according to special social or technical circumstances.

Governors are responsible for spending on salaries of all staff, including national insurance and superannuation; the day to day maintenance and costs of the premises, including rates and rent; and for books, equipment and other goods and services used by the school, including examination fees and insurance for items that are the school's responsibility.

All schemes must be fully operational by April 1993.

The money for education comes from local government (previously from rates, in the future from poll tax and business rate), from central government via the Rate Support Grant (which varies between local authorities according to government's view of local needs), and from charges for some services, like meals. Spending varies enormously from one LEA to another. For example, one LEA has one teacher for every 19.3 pupils in secondary schools, while in another not far away the secondary ratio is 1:13.3. This adds up to an enormous difference in spending.

Local councillors can allocate their total budget between different services. Once the education budget is set, the education committee, advised by the LEA officers, will decide how to spend it. Each year, spending plans start to be made in March for decisions made in September which will be implemented at the start of the financial year in April, finally reaching the schools in September. So ideally, governors should start to lobby for extra money for their schools 18 months in advance.

About 67 per cent of money spent directly on schools goes on employing teachers, and another 12 per cent on other staff. Repairs and maintenance take up 6 per cent, energy and water 4 per cent, rent and rates 4 per cent, books and equipment 5 per cent, home to school transport 1 per cent and other costs 1 per cent.

'Opting out'

Under the 1988 Act, schools can go even further down the road of self-government, and 'opt-out'.

Voluntary and county secondary schools with 300 or more pupils are eligible for a change to grant-maintained [GM] status ('opting out') if a majority of parents vote for it. The school will then be run by governors, who will be directly responsible to the Secretary of State, with the DES paying both recurrent and capital costs. The character of the school — for example whether it is grammar or comprehensive — can only be changed after an elaborate statutory procedure. Such changes will not normally be considered within five years of the school getting GM status.

The DES will withhold from the local authority the GM school's share of the schools budget, including its share of the 10 per cent that the LEA can keep back for central services.

The governing body can decide to hold a ballot of parents on opting out. If at least 20 per cent of parents make a written request to governors, they must arrange a ballot. If 50 per cent of all parents vote in the first ballot, and a majority is in favour of opting out, the governors must apply to the DES for grant-maintained status. If less than 50 per cent vote, a second ballot must be held within 14 days, and its results will be final, regardless of the numbers voting. Ballots will be carried out by the Electoral Reform Society, and paid for by the DES. The Secretary of State will then decide whether or not to grant GM status.

The governing body can decide, or 20+% of parents can demand, a ballot on opting out. There are strict rules on the procedure, which has been criticised on the ground that a fanatical minority can push through an 'opt out' if the majority do not vote. The newly-'opted out' school must have the right sort of governors for the Secretary of State to approve the change. 'First governors' — including local business people — must outnumber the rest.

Parents' rights

From September 1988 schools have been required to keep an up-to-date register of parents, usually meaning the people who have custody of the child, including non-custodial parents if known.

Parents have the right to have free education provided for their child from the beginning of the term after his or her fifth birthday up to the age of 19. They also have the right to choose to educate their child at home.

Parents may send their child to any school where there is a vacancy and where their child meets the admission criteria of the school. If they do not get a place at the school of their choice, they can appeal to an independent appeal committee, and they may take a friend to the appeal. If they are not satisfied with the conduct of the appeal, they may complain to the local ombudsman (county school appeals) or seek judicial review (voluntary schools).

Parents have a right to a free copy of the school prospectus, which must include information on many aspects of the life and work of the school — the hours of school sessions; the curriculum (shortly to include how the national curriculum subjects and religious education are organised, what other subjects are offered, and what qualifications pupils can gain); arrangements for sex education (if any); arrangements for homework and uniform; and the procedure for complaints.

In the future the school's aggregated results on national assessments at 11, 14 and 16, and possibly at 7, will also have to be included in the school prospectus.

Individual parents will shortly have to be given information about the syllabuses to be followed by their child. They will also have a right to know the educational achievements of their child on the national assessments, and to have information about the achievements of pupils at their school and at other schools. Parents will soon have the right to see the records or other information schools hold about their child, and any information about their child stored on computer. No information held by the school about their child may be shown to the police without parents' permission.

Parents will be able to complain to an independent body set up by the LEA, and afterwards to the Secretary of State, if they believe the governing body or LEA is acting unreasonably in not carrying out its responsibilities for the national curriculum or RE.

Parents have the right to consult with their child's teacher. Heads must keep parents informed about the school curriculum and the progress of their child.

Parents have the right to withdraw their children from religious education and the act of worship. They may withdraw their child at the beginning or end of the school day for religious instruction. They can also stop their child seeing the school doctor or dentist. They may withdraw their child for a maximum of two weeks in any school year for a family holiday. They may ask the governors for their child to be withdrawn from any sex education lessons, but the final decision is up to the governing body.

Parents have a right to free transport if they live sufficiently far from the school, and they have a right to free school meals if their income is low enough. They also have the right to provide their child with a packed lunch.

If their child is excluded from school, parents must be told the reason for the exclusion, when or if the child can return, and their right under certain circumstances to make representations to the governors and LEA. They must be informed about any directions of the governing body or the LEA about the exclusion. In the case of a permanent exclusion, parents must be informed about their right to appeal to an independent appeals committee. If they do appeal, they may take a friend with them to the appeal, if they wish.

Parents have a right to demand that the LEA makes an assessment as to whether or not their child has special educational needs. They must be involved in any assessment (whether proposed by themselves, the school or the medical services); to be told when their child will be examined; to say what, in their opinion, are the needs of the child and where s/he should be educated; and to see any draft statement of special needs prepared by the LEA. If the LEA decides not to make a statement, parents can appeal to the Secretary of State. Parents also have the right to insist that the LEA does not assess their child without their agreement.

Parent governors

Parents are involved in, and can be elected to, the governing body of a school.

Parents have the right to elect the specified number of parent governors to the governing body. The agenda for governors' meetings, and copies of any papers, must be available at the school for anyone interested to see, as must the draft minutes, as agreed by the chairperson of governors, after a meeting. (These are then replaced by the agreed minutes after the next governing body meeting.)

Governors must make an annual report to parents, and circulate it at least two weeks before the annual meeting for parents. It should include the date and place and agenda of the annual meeting; details of the members of the governing body and their term of office, and the name and address of the chairperson and the clerk; information about the next parent governor elections; a financial statement of money available to the school, and how it was spent; information about the curriculum, and the governors' policy where it modifies that of the LEA and about exam results in secondary schools.

In the future the annual report must also give information about the results for the national assessments at 11, 14 and 16 and possibly for 7-year-olds. The annual report should also mention the school's links with the community (including the police).

The annual meeting is supposed to give parents the opportunity to discuss the report and ask about the governors' work, and the work of the school and LEA. All parents must be informed about the meeting. The parents present may pass resolutions on any aspect of the school's or the LEA's work. Resolutions must be considered by the governing body and passed on to the head or the LEA if the matter is their responsibility.

Technically, for a resolution to be valid, the number of parents present at the meeting must be equal to at least 20 per cent of the number of registered pupils. But since so far not many annual meetings have attracted that many parents, most governing bodies consider all resolutions, and report back to parents.

LEAs have to decide the vexed question of who counts as a parent (step-parents, live-in partners, etc.) and give instructions to schools. All parents should know about the elections and how to be a candidate, and they must get a ballot paper and instructions on how to vote.

All parents should have a chance to meet candidates before the ballot takes place. (This can be an informal occasion to meet candidates one-to-one or in small groups: no meeting should test candidates' ability to handle a mass public meeting, which is not necessary for a good parent governor). All candidates should have the same opportunities to circulate a statement about themselves and (not necessary, but if anyone does it the chance should be given to all) a photograph. Arrangements in case of a tie for last place should be agreed beforehand: the normal method is to toss for it.

Governors' new responsibilities for monitoring the curriculum mean that some governors will have to develop a much more detailed knowledge of how the curriculum is planned and delivered in their school. Local management of schools, giving governors more direct responsibility for allocating resources, will make such knowledge even more essential. Possible tactics include attaching governors to specific departments and areas; asking for written or oral reports from subject departments or faculties; joint teacher–governor working groups on aspects of the curriculum; and formal 'visits' to departments, as well as reading school, LEA and national policy papers.

After the 1988 Act the LEAs' role on the curriculum is mainly to advise and to monitor standards. Their opportunities to promote curriculum development are now more limited, though they are still responsible for translating Government initiatives such as TVEI or Educational Support Grants into action.

Sex education and religious education

Sex and religion are reliable subjects for controversy where schools are concerned. The present position, under the 1988 Act, is that every school and sixth form college must offer religious education. RE has to be 'in the main' Christian, but can take account of other faiths represented in Britain. Each local authority is now required to have a Standing Advisory Council on Religious Education (SACRE), made up of representatives of Christian churches (and other faiths where appropriate), teachers, and the LEA. Its duty is to produce an agreed syllabus for RE, and to monitor its implementation in schools.

Each school must have an act of worship at some stage in the day for all pupils whose parents have not specifically asked for exemption. It must be 'wholly or mainly of a broadly Christian character'. Exceptionally a school may apply to the local SACRE for exemption from the 'broadly Christian' requirement if large numbers of pupils belong to other faiths. Parents have a right to withdraw their children from RE lessons and acts of worship.

The governing body of county schools have a responsibility to decide whether or not sex education should be taught in their school. If they decide it should, they must write and keep up-to-date a written statement outlining the content and organisation of sex education within their school. They can also decide whether parents should have the right to withdraw children.

Educational standards

The 'quality' of what goes on in schools has much exercised the Thatcher government and her Secretaries of State for Education, ironically, in view of their apparent inability to think with any depth or breadth about educational ideals. The measurement of quality is to be done in two ways: testing children against certain set standards at certain ages, and the use of 'performance indicators' for schools.

The tests will (largely) follow the advice of the government's Task Group on Assessment and Testing (TGAT), which has proposed a ten-point scale to cover the progress made by children of different abilities between ages 5 and 16. The jargon phrase is 'criterion-referenced tests', which measure what a child can do, rather than how his/her performance is ranked against that of other children.

For 7- to 11-year-olds, teachers will be able to choose from a bank of items from a child's topic work, as well as using traditional written question-and-answer tests. For 14-year-olds, the tests will probably be 'mini-GCSEs', by subject, and for 16-year-olds the GCSE will be the test.

Seven-year-olds in 1991 will be the 'guinea pigs'; those results will not be reported: the first proper testing will be in 1992. For 11-year-olds the first reported tests will be in 1995, and for 14-year-olds, 1993.

The TGAT's report was generally well-received — given that we had to accept the principle of testing — but we will have to wait and see whether the system works smoothly in practice. A very good question will be how much teacher-time and other resources the system uses up. Another concern, obviously, is to do with the reporting of results, presumably leading to invidious comparisons between schools, when a school with lower results may actually be doing better, given problems of language, special needs, and other factors outside the control of the teachers. TGAT recommended that results should be published only as part of 'a broader report by the school of its work as a whole'.

The discussions about broad 'performance indicators' for a school are in their early stages. An immense range of factors are important; some are easily measurable (cost per pupil, number of pupils obtaining a higher education place on leaving), others not (quality of leadership, quality of pastoral care). Of course, the main fear is of schools having to submit to an accountant's ruler exercise, with care and concern for people being lost sight of. Some of the suggestions have been bizarre: an objective measurement of how pupils look on the way to and from school was one serious idea! The whole area of how the performance indicators develop will be fascinating.

Individual pupils in certain schools, and across certain LEAs, have had 'profiles' — records of achievement — compiled about them during their secondary career. Often the pupil is actively involved, and proponents of the idea claim that it gives a more accurate picture of the pupil than exam results, offers continuous incentives to improve work and behaviour, and is welcomed by employers. It is expected that there will be a national system of pupil profiles by 1995.

Teachers' performances must be judged, following the 1986 Act, under a system known as 'appraisal'. There are, of course, those who regard this mainly as a way of weeding out bad (or subversive?) teachers, while the professional bodies aim to emphasise the opportunity to improve the quality of work.

Pupil behaviour

On how pupils are to be treated in schools, the head is responsible to the governors. At the extreme, if the head feels it necessary to exclude (the new word for suspend or expel) a pupil for more than five days, or if the period includes public examinations, the LEA and governors must be informed. The head can set conditions for return, such as referral to support services. Parents must be told of the exclusion, and the reasons, and they can appeal to an independent panel set up by the LEA. The LEA and governors can both override the head of a county school and order that a pupil, excluded indefinitely or permanently, be reinstated. In aided schools, only the governors can do this.

The support services that are involved in the case of problems are the Educational Welfare Officers (sometimes called Educational Social Workers) who liaise with families, and the Educational Psychologists, who help with behaviour *or* learning problems.

What is acceptable behaviour, of course, varies. Contrary to stories in the gutter press on newsless days, according to Her Majesty's Inspectorate serious discipline problems are rare. Good behaviour has to do with what some would say is good, green common sense: challenging teaching, active involvement of pupils, lots of positive reinforcement, and consistently applied, agreed values.

Research shows that the fewer the rules the better, and that negotiation and acceptance by pupils, with consistent application, lessen problems. Corporal punishment is now illegal: it will be interesting to see whether those schools that used it succeed in adopting more creative methods! Inappropriate sanctions still proliferate, and are often found to be a major part of disruption and alienation. Parents can, and should, ask questions at the appropriate meetings as to what the school policy is on sanctions, and then further, searching questions to tease out what actually happens.

Special needs

Pupils with 'special needs' are, following the 1981 Education Act, those who have particular learning difficulties significantly greater than their contemporaries, or a disability that prevents

them from participating normally. A parent, teacher, doctor or
health worker can ask for a child to be assessed by the LEA.
This may result in a 'statement of special educational needs'.
Parents have to be involved and can appeal, if necessary, to the
Secretary of State. 'Statementing' means that special provision
must be made as appropriate. Local provision, however, being
expensive and variable, the number of statemented children is
often related to the amount of provision available. If you are to
be born with special needs, you must choose carefully not only
your parents, but where you are born.

Equal opportunities

Equal Opportunities for all are, of course, enshrined in the law.
The Race Relations Act of 1976 and the Sex Discrimination Acts
of 1985 apply in schools as elsewhere. Girls, as girls, cannot be
excluded from an area of the curriculum or from an extra-curricular activity. Schools that care properly about these things either
have already introduced, or are doing so, policies on multiculturalism or anti-racism, and anti-sexism. The debate — often the
slanging match — between multiculturalism and anti-racism has
in my view been a painful waste of time, with some of the loudest
participants clearly seeming to me to have hidden agendas. There
are signs that the educational world is moving on to a creative
synthesis.

There is a very long way indeed to go: gross sexism and racism
may be disappearing, but the more dangerous, insidious kinds
are still alive and kicking among large numbers of teachers.
Awkward questions at meetings may be unwelcome, and schools
are institutionally very clever at deflecting them, but we will be
no nearer a green education, even with the correct curriculum
content, if school practices, procedures and attitudes do not
actively foster equal opportunity regardless of race or sex. The
EDC booklet and the book *Shattering Illusions* (see 'Resources')
will provide lots of ideas.

CHAPTER TWO
Roots of green education

Rene Descartes jumps out of bed with an idea and the scientific revolution is on its way.

The big question of the late sixteenth and early seventeenth centuries was, 'How can we do modern science?' They did not put it quite like that, but there had to be found new ways, at a time of rapid discovery, of thinking about and dealing with the physical world. The old ways of thinking just would not do: they were too narrow to allow the growth of the exciting new sciences, and they were fundamentally based on Authority, either classical or religious.

Rene Descartes (1596–1650), the man who wrote 'I think therefore I am' (though *not* any of the imitations), made the major contribution. He declared that we were to understand the world as if it is a great big clock. (This was the occasion of the jumping out of bed incident: Descartes claimed that the inspiration came to him in his sleep and out he jumped.) We must reduce the clock to the bits it is made of and understand the clock by understanding the bits. The scientist is to treat the phenomena of the natural world as quite separate from each other and quite separate from him or herself. These two ideas — reducing the world to study the bits, and treating the phenomena (bits) as separate (which included the parts of a person — mind and matter) — are called reductionism and dualism.

These two concepts have been enormously useful *and* have caused enormous harm. They allowed the seventeenth and eighteenth century scientific revolution to happen, by giving scientists both a way of thinking — a paradigm — and a way of guiding

19

their investigations. But they were so strong that holism — the assumption that we must treat people, and our physical world, as organic wholes, with non-physical matters being important — has had to struggle ever since. We are only now reclaiming, as the era of the scientific/industrial revolution comes to an end, the value, the values, inherent in the holistic approach to people and the earth.

One of the great ironies of our history is that some of the thinkers of the 'Enlightenment', a hundred years after Descartes, *both* strengthened the influence of dualism and reductionism *and* pointed to ways of treating people and the earth as rather more than agglomerations of separate bits.

John Locke's *Essay on Human Understanding* published in 1690 was one of the sparks that lit the fire that incinerated ways of thinking current since the Renaissance. The Enlightenment of which Locke was one of the fathers was a philosophical earth-quake. It was the flowering of open-ended, curious, rationally-based enquiry, asking, among other things, 'What do people need, and how can we freely organise our affairs to match those needs?'

Locke's *Some Thoughts Concerning Education* began as a series of letters to a friend, containing advice on the education of the friend's son. There are assumptions stated in the *Thoughts* that would not find favour today. One is that the education must contain physical 'hardening', for example making sure the boy was often cold and wet, as peasant children were, so that he could become as healthy as the peasants. Another is the strictly vocational nature of the education. Interestingly, this does not fit so easily with other, more far-sighted advice.

Locke gives as the four aims of education: wisdom, which the child cannot yet attain for lack of experience; breeding, or broadly, good manners ('not to think meanly'); virtue, or a fully developed moral sense, which Locke makes by far the most important: and learning, which Locke puts last in importance. It is clear that this was not orthodox at the time from Locke's description of it as a paradox, '[learning] being almost that alone which is thought of when people talk of education'.

This list, with or without the order of priorities, clearly fore-shadows holistic attitudes of later times. On methods of education, progressive attitudes were influenced by Locke:

He that hath found a way how to keep up a child's spirit easy, active and free, and yet at the same time to restrain him from many things he has mind to, and to draw him to things that are uneasy to him; he, I say, that knows how to reconcile these seeming contradictions, has, in my opinion, got the true secret of education.

He also anticipated the 'play-way' in education:

Children should not have anything like work, or serious, laid on them; neither their minds nor their bodies will bear it.

And

Were matters ordered right, learning anything they should be taught might be made as much a recreation to their play as their play is to their learning.

Stages of a curriculum should be attempted not at pre-set times, but only when the pupil is ready — 'the favourite seasons of aptitude and inclinations be heedfully laid hold of'.

Locke advocated an amazingly wide curriculum, including English (*not* considered essential, or even desirable as a subject, to strict classical educationists), French, Maths, History, Ethics, Law, Accounts, Science, Dancing, Singing, Gardening and Carpentry. I am certain that there are teacher-members of the Green Party reading this book now in whose school some at least of the students have a narrower curriculum than that!

He was one of the fathers of the liberal side of the eternal (it seems) nature–nurture argument: 'of all men we meet with, nine parts of ten are what they are, good or evil, useful or not, by their education. 'Tis that which makes the great difference in mankind.'

There has been disagreement about exactly how far Locke deserves sainthood in the green education heaven, but it is clear to me that, given the constraints of his own environment and times, this work of 300 years ago makes fascinating reading. I recommend that you take along your local library's copy of *Some Thoughts Concerning Education* to your next parents' meeting or open day: if the school passes muster on all major points it will be doing quite well, even in 1990!

Jean-Jacques Rousseau, who was much influenced by Locke, had the great good fortune with his most famous book on education, *Emile*, that it was condemned by the Archbishop of Paris to be burned and ordered to be torn and burnt by the Public Executioner. Any book which receives that welcome cannot be all bad. Burned in Paris could do for a French 18th century book what banned in Boston did for American novels in this century.

Meanwhile, Immanuel Kant, one of the half-dozen or so most influential philosophers in the history of the world, decided, for the only time in his life, not to go for his afternoon walk at exactly 3.30 pm on the day *Emile* arrived. He just had to read it through without stopping. Kant's judgement gives us an indication of the impact of the book:

> I am by disposition an inquirer. I feel the consuming thirst for knowledge, the eager unrest to advance even further, and the delights of discovery. There was a time when I believed that this is what confers real dignity upon human life, and I despised the common people who knew nothing. Rousseau has set me right. This imagined advantage vanishes, I learn to honour men, and should regard myself as of much less use than the common labourer, if I did not believe that my philosophy will restore to all men the common rights of humanity.

To be fair to the authorities, Rousseau *was* an extremely dangerous man: his 'Social Contract' ('Man is born free but is everywhere in chains . . .') was to undermine the old regime with fatal consequences for very many people: the French Revolution was a bloody business.

Rousseau's work was a passionate response to the horrors of materialism as it was emerging as the dominant ethos in the eighteenth century.

As well as being credited with (or blamed for) the French Revolution, and with having a crucial influence on libertarian movements ever since, Rousseau has also been the strongest influence on the liberal, child-centred and holistic education movements. It was Rousseau who insisted that there be no preset curriculum: it should emerge as the child develops, based on experiental learning and discovery. It was Rousseau who most fully developed the ideas of Locke and others that the different stages of childhood were each unique, that they required different aims and modes of education, and that they should each be enjoyed to the full by the child before he or she was moved on to the next.

The aim of education was to be liberty and happiness, within whatever constraints were unavoidable. Rousseau has been blamed for some of the sillier experiments in freedom in education, but what he advocates has been extremely useful to those educators prepared to think seriously about the relationship between freedom and responsibility. 'Self-knowledge and self-control, the arts of life and happiness.' Education was to 'follow the order of nature'. Rousseau's basic problem was how, having decided that the child is by nature good and beautiful and pure, to devise an education that shielded the child from, *and* prepared him for, life in society. Society, artificial, materialistic, and destructive of human and spiritual values, was not to be avoided for ever. Education was to develop in and for the child a harmony, reconciling the needs of human development and the requirements of the social contract.

Following the order of nature did not mean, as some critics — and followers — have thought, sentimentalising the child and leaving everything to unguided, spontaneous accident. It meant recognising the child's 'endowment' from nature, the innate tendencies, and respecting them.

The importance of 'following the order of nature' was to do with the unity between the rational principle and the governing of the universe by divine providence. Human reason — the only way of dealing with ideas about virtue, which is the foundation of all aims of education — was ultimately a spiritual matter: it came from nature, whose ultimate principle is spiritual. This is what separates, from the 1760s to the 1990s, the two families of the children of the Age of Reason (and we are all that). For some, rationality is linked with a mechanistic world view — everything can be explained as if it is part of a physical machine, including the human being. For others, influenced by Rousseau, we can abandon traditional religiosity but still insist on the 'secret heart': the idea that the natural endowment of every person is an inner being connected to the universal source of life.

It is this that makes holistic, green educators say that we cannot explain human beings in terms of the machine. It could never account for what is important: creativity, self-renewal, the fact that the whole human being is infinitely greater than the sum of his biological parts. In the late twentieth century, green educators are struggling to put these beliefs into practice — and often succeeding. So, as paradigms shift, children will be better prepared to cope, not just intellectually and practically but with *all* their faculties.

What has come to be known in the twentieth century as progressive education came to us from Rousseau via a great number of routes, not all of which, alone, would have led in the directions taken in recent times.

At the end of the eighteenth century, and early in the nineteenth (he died in 1827), Johann Heinrich Pestalozzi was running a series of experiments in schooling according to his ideas, and was writing a series of books attempting to explain them. Neither the experiments nor the books were entirely — in some cases at all — successful, but the stream of distinguished visitors who came to visit him in Switzerland spread his fame throughout Europe. While some parents and tutors elsewhere were applying Rousseauite ideas to individual pupils, Pestalozzi was struggling to develop ways of using them in running a school. It was his demonstration that this is possible that allowed Rousseau to be a major influence in elementary schooling later in the century in both Europe and America.

Friedrich Froebel (1782–1852) visited Pestalozzi's school at Yverdon and was not greatly impressed. The difference between the powerful inspiration of Pestalozzi's ideas and the disappointment, especially after excited anticipation, of what was actually happening can be seen in Froebel's words in 1810:

> The powerful, indefinable, stirring and uplifting effect produced by Pestalozzi when he spoke, set one's soul on fire for a higher, nobler life. . . . On the whole I passed a glorious time at Yverdon, elevated in tone, and critically decisive for my after life. At its close, however, I felt more clearly than ever the deficiency of inner unity and interdependence, as well as of outward comprehensiveness and thoroughness in the teaching there.

What is today regarded as obvious, just simple good practice with young children — learning by doing, dealing with real things — came to us largely from Pestalozzi's principle of *Anschauung*: spontaneous appreciation based on concrete experience. And what is a large part of what many mean by holism in education today was handed on by another aspect of Pestalozzi's work:

> God's nature which is in you is held sacred in this House. We do not hem it in; we try to develop it. Nor do we impose on you our own natures. It is far from our intention to make of you men such as we are. It is equally far from our intention to make of you such men as are the majority of men in our time. Under our guidance

you should become men such as your natures — the divine and sacred in your nature — require you to be.

Friedrich Froebel was strongly influenced by those German philosophers who were urgently seeking a way of understanding the problem of existence, of nature, as a unity. Part of the dedication of his book *The Education of Man* reads:

> The whole world — the All, the Universe — is a single great organism in which an eternal uniformity manifests itself. This principle of uniformity expresses itself as much in external nature as in spirit. Life is the union of the spiritual with the material. Without mind or spirit matter is lifeless; it remains formless, it is mere chaos. Only through the entrance of the spiritual into the material does the cosmos originate. Spirit manifests itself in order. Every creature, every object is matter informed by spirit.

Whether or not we interpret this as the traditional Christian God — as Froebel elsewhere seems to do — it is clear that we have here another link in a developing chain.

Froebel invented the *Kindergarten*. A wonderful indication that this new new institution — because of the ideas behind it — was regarded as really subversive is the fact that *Kindergartens* were banned in Prussia in 1851 as dangerous to society! Froebel saw early childhood as 'the most important stage of the total development of man and humanity'.

> The earliest age is the most important one for education because the beginning decides the manner of progress and the end. If national order is to be recognised in later years as a benefit, childhood must first be accustomed to law and order, and therein find means of freedom.

Froebel made much of his famous 'gifts' to the child — firstly the soft ball, and secondly the sphere, the cube and the cylinder. He wrote some outlandish things about how the small child understands the convoluted psychological symbolism of these play items. They are too silly to quote here, but what was important — and has remained — is a system of education that in the hands of good teachers has benefitted enormous numbers of children, and still does.

The other well-known pioneer of progressive education with small children, Maria Montessori (1870–1952) worked in very different ways from Froebel. His *Kindergarten* had been in a wealthy, rural valley. Montessori's 'House of Childhood' was in the slums of Rome. Froebel's work centred on the 'natural environment' and development of the child, Montessori's emphasised the environment around the child.

Montessori's work arose out of early pioneering work in public housing. An 'Association of Good Building' acquired tenements in the poorest parts of Rome, rehabilitated them and handed them over to the tenants. The scheme worked well but there was a problem of graffiti and minor vandalism with the small children. Montessori was brought in, in 1906, as a teacher who would enable the children to spend their time more usefully. She had developed her ideas about education while working with 'mentally defective' children, and reckoned that her methods would work well with normal ones.

By the early twentieth century the 'psychological method' — meaning the adaptation of each stage of education to the stage of development of the child, and his/her interests, rather than some pre-determined curriculum or a teacher's scheme of work — was established, and Montessori based her methods on her understanding of it. Each child is free to develop according to his/her needs at the time: each child has independence of action. The atmosphere, the environment is so ordered that independent action brings about development:

> Give the child an environment in which everything is constituted in proportion to himself and let him live therein. Then there will develop within the child that 'active life' which has caused so many to marvel because they see in it not only a simple exercise performed with pleasure but also the revelation of a spiritual life.

Various aspects of Montessori work have changed in recent years but she is crucial, in this short story, for two reasons. The teaching of young children is strongly influenced to this day by the range of practical activities which her methods introduced, and, more importantly, her individualisation of teaching — trying to cater for the individual needs of each particular child at all times — was credited with sounding the 'death knell' of the old-style class-teaching. Not, of course, that it is dead yet, but the fact that it is used so much less than in the old elementary school days is largely due to the influence of Maria Montessori.

John Dewey's life almost coincided with Montessori's:

1859–1952. He was the most influential educationist of the twentieth century, partly because his educational work was part and parcel of his wider philosophical work. He has been called the philosopher of the liberal democratic way of life, and, for him, participation became the watchword of education. Not wanting to set up grand theories, new or otherwise, he insisted on a pragmatic approach: education should progress by using the experimental, scientific method. Experience, gained from experiments based simply on certain 'essentials' — the 'eternal realities which do not change and the beauties which do not fade' — would show the way forward.

There has been controversy about whether Dewey was as pragmatic, as against theory, as he claimed, and about whether the pragmatic approach was proven in any case. Also, the 'child-centred' branch of the progressive movement, or some sections of it, were criticised by Dewey for exaggerating his views on students' freedom. And those holistic educators who base their views on belief in an *actual* divine aspect to human nature, rather than a metaphorical one, as Dewey did, have had their doubts about him.

But Dewey's work was — is — extremely influential on both sides of the Atlantic, in *both* the child-centred and the holistic movements. He reinforced the tradition of learning by doing, he established finally that big-scale education systems can educate children as children and not as future adults, and began the final assault on the old 'static cold-storage ideal of knowledge'. He is also probably the most profound influence on our thinking about the link between education and democracy. He was concerned with the problem of 'how do you educate for democracy?' — as we are still — and the moves in the twentieth century in the direction of having a democratic form of education, at all levels including that of the student, owe him a lot. He pointed out, especially in the USA, after World War I, that democratic education was more and more needed, to counteract the evils of overdeveloped capitalist competition and greed.

While the 'social reconstructionists' in the USA and the Fabians and others in Britain were developing the ideas of Dewey as a way of humanising a materialist, science-based society, others were more ambitious.

The 'modern school' of the Spanish anarchist Francisco Ferrer was a constant source of romantic ideas and influence in the USA from the time of Ferrer's execution in 1909 to the 1950s.

Ferrer had written: 'We want men who will continue unceasingly to develop; men who are capable of constantly destroying and renewing their surroundings and renewing themselves. . . . Society fears such men; you cannot expect it to set up a system of education which will produce them.'

No wonder he had to be got rid of. *Progressive Education* magazine in 1930 showed the movement's discontent with the process of accommodating to current values: 'We are tired of facts, persons in the mass, things, propaganda, social and economic classifications, standardisation. . . . We are talking about the person as an end in himself, his individuality, not of an economic factor in society.'

Meanwhile another holistic educator had emerged, who — if these things are measured by the number of schools founded — is extremely important in this story. Rudolf Steiner (1861–1925) has inspired the founding of a large number of schools in Britain today and many more in America and continental Europe. The root of his philosophy was that: 'there slumber in every human being faculties by means of which he can acquire for himself a knowledge of higher worlds. Mystics, Gnostics, theosophists — all speak of a world of soul and spirit which for them is just as real as the world we see with our physical eyes and touch with our physical hands.'

Steiner believed that Western scientific materialism had made it difficult for people to know about the spiritual core of their reality, and he is certainly not alone in this. Education should be done with the specific aim of assisting the process of penetrating this core, and allowing the unfolding of the spiritual essence, alongside the development of all the 'gifts' a person possesses.

Steiner — or Waldorf as it is known elsewhere — teaching is not totally child-centred because the teachers have a predetermined set of ideals and a predetermined set of practices and procedures. But an awe at 'the creative power within the human soul', and the overriding aim of self-awakening within the child have led many educators in recent years, whose impulses are green in the sense this book uses, to give support to Steiner-inspired schools. How much Steiner has influenced teachers and schools in the regular system is another question. Many people do have a problem with the adherence of Steiner schools to a single, quasi-religious, or certainly narrowly defined, set of spiritual beliefs. But Steiner is worth a close look for anyone exploring alternatives.

The best-known progressive school in Britain, probably, is Summerhill. A. S. Neill (1883–1973), who founded and ran Summerhill, based his ethos of freedom (schools like Summerhill were sometimes called free schools — confusingly, as they were not entirely free educationally and were often extremely expensive financially) on two grounds. The first was the need of the child to escape the psychoanalytic problems of repression. The second was his belief — he said his experience — that children given almost unlimited opportunity to test their natural impulses did develop the desire to learn and to become constructive citizens, of the school and of outside society.

Neill was not overly starry-eyed about the operation of self-government at Summerhill. He was criticised *both* on the ground that it was a sham, *and* that there was too much of it. Many progressive schools have had the kind of problems Neill describes here when 'old-stagers', who have learned to use freedom, are joined by students for whom it is a new, and dangerous, toy:

Is your self-government phoney? David Holbrook would seem to think it's no good.

David Holbrook in an article in *Id*, the journal of the Summerhill Society writes: 'I think of the children sitting on the floor of Neill's school voting on their own rules: in a way this is asking children to do what the adults should do for them.' David was sixteen when he last saw a school meeting.

I do not know where to begin with this criticism, for it reaches down to fundamentals. It questions self-regulation in general. It really asks: how far can a child decide social matters for itself? We all know the other way, the usual way. . . . Your elders know better, so do as you are told. Some of us ask if elders do know better. In Summerhill I know better about some things. I don't ask the pupils to appoint a teacher; Ena does not ask what food they shall have. I decide about fire escapes, Ena about health rules. We buy and repair the furniture; we decide what textbooks should be bought. None of these factors come into self-government. Nor do the pupils want them to. Self-government to them means dealing with situations that arise in their communal life; they can say what they like, vote how they like in a meeting, and they never wait to see how the staff votes. True a member of the staff can often get his or her motion carried, but the motion is judged on its merits. I have proposed scores of motions in my time and had them outvoted. We never ask children to decide on things that are beyond their ability to grasp.

Good self-government arises when we have a goodly sprinkling of older pupils, but they should be pupils who have grown up in the system. When we enrol boys and girls of fifteen and over they do not help the self-government; they have too many repressions to let off, they do not grasp freedom unconsciously as adolescents do who have had seven or eight years in the school. So that sometimes today our government has too much of the staff element in it. If someone throws food all over the dining-room walls an older pupil will raise the matter in a meeting, that is if he or she is an old stager, but recently when we had an influx of teenagers who had no social feeling about food throwing, one of the staff would bring the matter up. We all feel that this is bad, but under the circumstances, inevitable.

Self-government is maybe phoney when there are only young children. Since we began with five children we learned the hard way that very young children have not the ability to make rules impartially, yet the strange feature is that all the very young kindergarten ones come to every meeting and register their votes, and often make good speeches before they can read and write.

What part should adults play in self-government? They should not lead; they should have the gift of standing more or less outside. When a child is charged with some breach of the rules I make it a point never to vote for or against — say — a sixpenny fine. I sometimes have to have a private talk with a pupil (a P.L.) and it would be impossible for me to vote that Willie be fined for riding Tom's bike, and then be his therapist next day.

I think the test of the value of self-government lies in the determination of the pupils to retain it. Any suggestion of abolishing it, even of limiting its powers is met by a very strong reaction. I have suggested abolition twice but would not dare ever to do so again.

I grant that democracy is far from perfect. Majority rule is not too satisfactory, but I can see no alternative barring dictatorship. The minority always suffers. What has surprised me for years has been that our school minority accepts the majority verdict; if there is a refusal to accept it it comes from some lad of fifteen who has just come and cannot see why he has to obey 'what a crowd of bloody kids vote on'.

Is the whole set-up phoney in that children make laws and don't keep them? Some laws are often broken, especially the bedtime law, yet I am sure that if I made the laws more of them would be broken, for then the natural rebellion against father would come in. In a fear boarding school there is law-breaking in the dormitories at nights. 'The Law makes the crime.'

On the whole the laws in Summerhill are pretty well kept, partly, maybe mainly, because children are so charitable with each other. I have marvelled for forty-five years about the sense of justice they show. A boy is charged for bullying and reprimanded by the meeting. At the next meeting he brings up a trumpery charge against the bullyee. The meeting spots that it is a revenge charge and tells him so.

Someone wrote that our self-government is a fake because the staff really makes the rules and pretends that the pupils make them by a show of hands. That is just a libel as any pupil, past or present, would know. As I have said many a time they will vote for a law on its own merits whoever proposes it. I have more than once proposed that the loud gram be played only in the evenings. I am always outvoted. One of the staff will bring up the wastage of good food . . . we have a tuckshop just outside the grounds, and often a child will stoke up on ice lollies and come to lunch and leave it. The staff proposal may be that anyone leaving his or her lunch should be deprived of lunch next day. The motion is never carried. Again and again I have proposed that money sent to pupils during term should be pooled and divided equally. This is always negatived; all the ones with the least pocket money from home vote against it. But I have said enough to show that our democracy is not fake I hope.

The next extract may unfortunately reinforce the popular prejudice that sex reared its ugly head at Summerhill (and progressive schools in general) alarmingly frequently, but it is worth quoting for what it says of Neill's confidence in the results of freedom:

In my school I have never attempted to get children to share my beliefs or my prejudices. . . .

I have no religion but have never taught one word against religion, nor against the barbarous criminal code, nor anti-Semitism, nor imperialism. I have never influenced children to become pacifists or vegetarians or temperance reformers. My propaganda is a subtle one; I know that preaching cuts no ice with children, so I put my trust in the power of freedom to fortify youth against sham and fanaticism and isms of any kind. Yes, I leave freedom to counteract organized propaganda for what, to me, are evil things . . . not meaning that pacifism and vegetarianism, etc. are evil of course. But when my daughter of six came to me and said: 'Willie has the biggest cock among the small kids, but Mrs X (a visitor) says it is rude to say cock,' I at once told her volubly that it was not rude, and inwardly cursed the woman for her ignorant and narrow understanding of children. I might tolerate propaganda from other people about politics or manners, but when anyone attacks my own child or any other child, making it guilty about sex, I bring all my batteries into action and fight back vigorously. Put it this way: propaganda for — say — a political theory may and will affect the child emotionally, but propaganda by Mrs Grundy goes straight to the solar plexus. A child can grow out of being a Labourite or a Tory or a Communist, but the life-hating prejudices of a sex obsessionist are likely to open up the way to a neurotic adulthood. Politics may start in the emotions but in the end the intellect comes into play; with a Mrs Grundy repression the intellect cannot influence what fixed firmly in the solar plexus.

The advocates of propaganda say something like this: There is a vast amount of subtle propaganda that must affect the children — the pornographic laugh in the cinema, the hush-hush about birth, the press with its reports of crimes, the news reels with their glorification of tanks and bombs, the magistrates with their moral lectures. Is it fair to children to let the devil play them all the worst tunes? I answer cheerfully that if you preserve your child from guilt, especially guilt about its body and its sex, it will come almost unscathed through the most dangerous barrage of moral and sinister big guns. I say *almost* unscathed and that 'almost' is what makes me keep a sharp eye on the Grundy woman.

Very few British teachers in the last thirty years will have got through college without at least hearing something of Neill and Summerhill. It might be interesting to ask how, if at all, that movement has influenced them!

Dartington in Devon, founded in 1925, was another well-known example of the progressive school movement. It was part of a wider social experiment to revive arts and crafts and rural life, and during its life achieved at various times work of such quality that it was seen as inspirational from all round the world. One continuing legacy is the annual Dartington Conference, which maintains the tradition of attempting to integrate the intellectual, the emotional and the spiritual in the service of holistic education. Its later years were difficult, when the necessary relationships between freedom, responsibility and self-discipline became strained, under outside influences. Again, as with Summerhill, major problems were caused by the school's accepting students who, 'corrupted' by conventional society, found freedom extremely difficult to handle. The school closed in 1984.

Summerhill, Dartington and many other new schools were profoundly influenced by Homer Lane. He founded and ran a reformatory in Detroit, USA, where he gave the boys a great deal of self-government, came to Britain, and in 1913 established the 'Little Commonwealth' in Dorset. Here, delinquent boys and girls were paid for their work, and operated, for themselves, their own system. There were 'no rules and regulations except those made by the boys and girls themselves. All citizens of the Commonwealth attend courts, and the highest judicial authority is the referendum. Disputed points as between the citizen, judge and an offender are decided by public opinion by means of the roll-call.'

Schools all over Britain were experimenting in the 1920s with these exciting ideas — County Senior Schools and even Rugby — after a book by Percy Nunn, *Education: Its Data and First Principles*, had publicised them. I wonder how far, seventy years on, schools in your area feel able to allow the students the opportunity to develop as self-governing democrats? In my experience the very thought, if allowed to go beyond a facile, nominal School Council, scares the pants off a headteacher even faster than most other educational innovations calculated to undermine the mega-machine.

The 1960s and early 1970s were times of enormous optimism and change, in education as in other spheres. Education students were reading authors like Paul Goodman, whose *Growing Up Absurd* had in 1960 offered an examination of 'Youth in the Organised Society', looking at 'the disgrace of the Organised System, of semi-monopolies, government, advertisers, and the disaffection of the growing generation'. In his other well-known book of 1962, *Compulsory Miseducation*, he warns of how society continually uses progressive education as something which naturalises, humanises 'each new social and technical development' — so that we are always having to deal with a horrible new twist of the materialist–industrialist ratchet, never able to 'grow naturally into the future'. We must make sure we get ahead of this bind. The mega-machine gobbling up, digesting and defæcating again.

At the end of *Compulsory Miseducation*, Goodman says:

These are a few speculations of one mind. My purpose is to get people at least to begin to think in another direction, to look for an organization of education less wasteful of human resources and social wealth than what we have. In reconstructing the present system, the right principles seem to me to be the following: To make it easier for youngsters to gravitate to what suits them, and to provide many points of quitting and return. To cut down the loss of student hours in parroting and forgetting, and the loss of teacher hours in talking to the deaf. To engage more directly in the work of society, and to have useful products to show instead of stacks of examination papers. To begin to decide what should be automated and what must not be automated, and to educate for a decent society in the foreseeable future.

To be candid, I do not think that we will change along these lines. Who is for it? The suburbs must think I am joking, I understand so little of status and salary. Negroes will say I am downgrading them. The big corporations like the system as it is, only more so. The labour unions don't want kids doing jobs. And the new major class of school-monks has entirely different ideas of social engineering.

Nevertheless, in my opinion, the present system is not viable; it is leading straight to 1984, which is not viable. The change, when it comes, will *not* be practical and orderly.

The pessimistic view would be that, today, the mega-machine has in fact gobbled up the advances, such as they were, of the sixties and seventies, in just the way Goodman warned, without the violent reaction, even after 1984, that he foresaw.

But there have been advances, there are grounds for hope. The right-wing backlash, officially sponsored in both Britain and the USA, has met much teacher-resistance. The messages of the humanistic psychologists, developing further, with notions of 'self-actualisation', what progressive/holistic educators have been saying since Rousseau, have been getting through. They form the bulk of the syllabus at various teacher-training institutions. New work on brain function — left brain and right brain, and the problems linked with over- or under-using one or the other — is finding its way into the public consciousness. Some, even, of the recent changes imposed by the Thatcher government in Britain are based on at least lip-service to old progressive ideals that they think they can use — more self-guided discovery, in GCSE project work and in TVEI; the core curriculum, making sure everyone has a more rounded, complete experience; greater devolution of financial decision-making power to the school; greater parental and community involvement in the governing of the school. I freely admit one does have to strain a little to be optimistic, but it is possible! Radical environmental education is growing, peace education is maturing and developing after an exciting upsurge in the early eighties, development education is a growth area. And, most importantly, the teachers in these areas recognise the links between the areas: holism at this level is strong. *Green Teacher* magazine flourishes; the Centre for Alternative Technology's education services are inundated by teachers wanting to bring students. 'Teaching green' lives!

We do know, as the mega-machine marches on and becomes even more dangerous and apparently all-powerful, that what we do in the greening of education is rooted in a long, vigorous tradition, recently enormously strengthened. If we take confidence from this tradition, we can gain ideas and inspiration from some of the items that appear in the rest of this book. Then we can begin, or carry on, reducing the destructiveness of the mega-machine, and then, perhaps, our children can lay the groundwork for life after its demise.

CHAPTER THREE
The system emerges

On a pessimistic reading of 200 years of education history, we are about to see, again, the fruits of an enormous flowering of human enlightenment swallowed up and perverted by the mega-machine. It does seem that this has always happened; it can seem that, given the occasional naïvety of the proponents of the greening of education, and the cleverness and power of the high priests of the mega-machine, the old process will repeat itself.

One of the major characteristics of green thinking is its belief that it contains seeds of future life so new and unique and vital to the next stage of human evolution that it is bound to become the new conventional wisdom sooner or later. That or eco-catastrophe and the end of all wisdoms, conventional or otherwise. Eco-catastrophe aside (would that it were so easy!), a short look at the period 1790 to 1990 should help make sure we don't become complacent.

The eyes and ears of the mega-machine are long-practised in perceiving the importance of life-enhancing philosophical movements and pretending to ignore them, while watching them, ready to defeat them. Its jaws are skilled at snapping off their heads — literally in some personal cases, and just as effectively in all others. Its guts have all the acid juices and destructive bacteria required to ensure that, after the process of digestion and defaecation, the original hopeful ideals bear the same relationship to the eventual outcome as that between a beautiful meal and the steaming pile of waste products. But we can think of the same ecological principles applying to the food cycle and to the cycle of educational ideas. The waste products of one stage of the process — manure, or the apparently spent ideals of reformers — feed the next one.

The high hopes of the sixties for comprehensivisation, of equal treatment for all, of radical improvements in quality of provision, along with democratisation of the system, allowing education to engineer a deepening of our democracy, all look a bit sad now.

But in the eternal ecological way of ideals, they will — have already started to — feed the next great move, in the green direction.

The demands in the 1960s for comprehensivisation — which, like most educational 'innovations', was not as new as its opponents, and even some of its enthusiasts, believed — arose largely from disappointment with the post–1944 system. This system, with its grammar schools, technical schools and modern schools for pupils of differing supposed needs, arose from the genuine belief that the enlightened use of psychology — tests of ability and aptitude — could scientifically put each child in the right place. This belief was accompanied by the conviction that the new system was, in the words of the Norwood Report 'in accordance with the principle of child-centred education'.

Combine all that with the enormous improvements being made at the same time in child-care law and anti-poverty welfare rights, and we can see that the new, *free* secondary education for all marked the dawn of a new era. That it failed the hopes of its enthusiasts and was used and abused by the mega-machine should not, in retrospect, surprise us. Nor should the fact that from its discredited, steaming remains has developed the present set-up which, for all its faults, is a long way forward in social justice, in academic *and* non-academic standards of performance, and in possibilities for further advance. Whether that advance will be facilitated or delayed by central government we will have to wait and see: the record of the 1980s Conservative government is appalling, though some of its reforms can be used subversively.

Governments are not the mega-machine: they simply form a more or less substantial part of it, and/or give more or less help to it, at different times. For most of the last 200 years governments have had little direct hand in what went on in schools, though of course they contributed to the cycle of reform and disappointment by legislation, or lack of it, and by finance, or lack of it.

As Britain was industrialising in the late eighteenth and early nineteenth centuries, there was rapid development of ideas about education, and about systems of education, in response to the enormous social changes which were happening more quickly than ever before. The emergent ruling class of industrial capitalists contained many who feared that political revolution could follow industrial revolution unless education was used, along with the army and repressive laws, to produce a submissive workforce.

Others were more confident and allowed themselves slightly higher ideals in supporting education, and the liberal tendency was strongly influenced by radical ideas about education. These ideas had been crucial in the work of the philosophers who influenced the French Revolution. Britain's first working class political organisations, the Corresponding Societies, enthusiastically drew inspiration from the new idea that *all* people were educable, and believed that social and political progress would be built on the basis of educational work. In Tom Paine's *The Rights of Man*, Mary Wollstonecraft's *A Vindication of the Rights of Woman*, and William Godwin's *Political Justice*, education, human rights and social progress are inextricably linked.

The doctrine of utilitarianism — the pursuit of the greatest good of the greatest number — acted, despite *laissez-faire* economics, as underpinning for the view that the people should be educated. But this secular theory concentrated on the idea of education for a social role: to work or to govern. Moreover, it was strongly echoed by the church groups, who advocated education for the purpose of producing working people who would defer to traditional religious/moral teachings, and accept the social order.

Anyone who still believes that the Methodists carried religious dissent into the desire for political dissent via education for democracy should read E. P. Thompson's *The Making of the English Working Class*.

While much was being written, and plans being dreamed, about mass education as a social force, the ideas of Rousseau were being applied by a small number of English enthusiasts. Rousseau, we have seen, had had a fundamental influence on the radicalism of this time, fostering the belief that each person was pure and good, and that the correct education allowed as 'natural' a development as possible, unsullied by society. Individual experiments had no luck.

One hopeful, Thomas Day, applied Rousseauite methods to two orphan girls in the hope of producing a perfect wife (what would have happened to the other is one of many good questions!). Another, R. L. Edgeworth, tried to demonstrate that the methods worked on his son. The unfortunate girls were judged failures and were married off to other husbands and the boy ran wild and was sent to boarding school. Many radicals, including romantics, were critical of the intense, protected regime of the Rousseau child. Wordsworth was contemptuous of those who set themselves up as

> . . . keepers of our time,
> The guides and wardens of our faculties,
> Sages who in their prescience would control
> All accidents. . . .
>
> *The Prelude*, BOOK V

But the cult of the innocence and wisdom of the child, whose natural freedom, beauty and purity must be revered and protected, grew with the work of Wordsworth, Blake, Coleridge and others: child as depraved was out!

So the early nineteenth century demands for educational progress came from an odd mixture of concern for the individual free child, concern for moral and religious conformity, concern for industrial skills and political submission, and concern for social and political progress via an educated democracy. Does this sound familiar? It was possible for the idealists to be optimistic. But what happened?

One answer is that the Sunday School movement, begun in the 1780s, grew rapidly. 2.4 million children were on their registers in 1851. Hannah More, the most famous of the religious tract-writers (her works sold 2 million copies in 1795 alone) stated the purpose of the Sunday Schools clearly: 'To train up the lower classes in habits of industry and piety.' She considered the teaching of writing to poor children to be quite unnecessary, as did the Wesleyans. It was only in Wales, where some self-governing, democratic congregations provided worship, discussion and elementary Welsh education for children and adults, that ambitions were perhaps higher, and that Sunday Schools had some limited social and political significance.

The main response to the early nineteenth century mix of idealism and cynicism was the monitorial system. This applied the principles of utilitarian philosophy and industrial efficiency to the education of poor children, and had the enormous advantage of being cheap. The British and Foreign School Society, founded in 1808, grew out of the work of Joseph Lancaster, a Quaker, who had opened a school in 1798 and developed his 'arrangements for the education . . . [of poor children] . . . at a very trifling expense to the public'. The Church of England responded by founding the National Society, to provide schooling based on the very similar principles of Dr Andrew Bell.

The principles involved a small number of pupils being given the job of monitor. A monitor would act as a sort of junior officer, passing on instructions and drilling small groups —normally about ten, but up to twenty — of other children. These would usually be younger, but could be as old as the monitor. Throughout the day, monitors would be either 'teaching' their groups while the master conducted mass writing exercises with the rest of the class, or receiving instruction, later to be passed on, from the teacher. Rewards — prizes of medals or cash (e.g. best boy of the week, a halfpenny) — and punishments (e.g. confinement in a closet or a suspended basket, or a pillory, being washed in public or wearing the fool's cap) regulated each establishment in a more or less orderly manner.

The system worked extremely well, in conferring 'upon the Children of the Poor the Inestimable Benefit of Religious Instruction, combined with such other Acquirements as may be suitable to their Station in Life, and calculated to render them useful and respectable Members of Society'. Endowed schools and public schools all over the country copied the monitorial system in one way or another, especially in the 1830s and 1840s. Something of the flavour of the 'System of Primary Instruction' is seen below in the extract from the Manual (for teachers) of the British and Foreign School Society of 1831.*

Vocabulary of Commands and Order of Occupation
The following are the usual commands, which may be communicated either visibly or audibly.

Nine o'clock
The school commences. The children, on entering, proceed to their desks, and the master reads a chapter from the Bible, the boys remaining perfectly quiet.

Fifteen minutes past nine
The training of the monitors: the mass of the school writing on slates. Preparatory to writing, the general monitor of order would say 'Recover'; the boys bring their hands to the string of the slates — 'Slates' shown up, 'Lay down slates', as expressed — 'Clean Slates'; the writing is rubbed out — 'Hands'; they cease rubbing the slate —

---

*Reprinted in J. Lawson and H. Silver, *A Social History of England*, (Methuen, London 1973).

'Down'; they sit prepared for writing — 'Eighth class monitor begin'; a word is dictated for his class to write.

Forty-five minutes past nine
The boys would be exercised out to their reading drafts. The following commands would be given by the master or general monitor. 'Hands'; the boys clap on the desks, 'Down', 'Clean', 'Slates'. The writing is then rubbed out. 'Hands', 'Down', 'Look'; the boys then observe the hand of the general monitor, and turn in the direction he moves it in. 'Out'; the boys jump out. 'Front'; they then face the platform. 'Look'; the general monitor turns in the direction of their reading draft stations. 'Go'; they are then led to their drafts by the class monitors, either quite quietly, or repeating their tables.

Eleven o'clock
The general monitor says aloud, 'Stop reading' — 'Turn' — 'Go'; they are then led by the monitors back to their desks. . . . The general monitor of arithmetic then says 'Cipherers — front'; (the boys face the platform), 'Recover' (they clap on the desks), 'Slates', they unstring the slates, and lodge them against the screw on the desk. 'Show slates', they then turn in the direction of his hand. 'Go' and they are then led to their ciphering drafts.

Twelve o'clock
The school is dismissed. The commands for this are 'Sling'; each boy touches the slate sling with his left hand, and the lower end of his slate with his right hand. 'Slates'; each is lifted over the upper end of the desk and suspended. 'Hands down' — 'Look' — 'Turn' — 'Out'; they jump out of the seats and stand. 'Front'; they face the monitor, 'Unsling'; bring up the fingers of both hands to the strings which fasten their hats to the backs. 'Hats'; untie the strings and place the hats on the desks. 'Put on hats', 'Hands behind', 'Look' — they are then turned in the direction of the doors. 'Go'; led out quietly, or repeating tables. A class of elder boys, of from twenty to thirty, would remain behind to receive additional and personal instruction from the teacher.

We know amazingly little about the quality of teaching, progressive or otherwise, or the breadth of the curriculum, in monitorial schools in general. Harold Silver reports his and his colleagues' surprise to find 'a more imaginative and human approach to children and to school affairs, and stronger school–community links than we had expected, or could explain'. With Pamela Silver, he studied the history of a Church school for the poor in Kennington, and found that it was a leader in public health work; there was a record of humanity and innovation, apparently continuously, from its creation in 1824. We do know that the main problem was a severe shortage of high quality teachers, and that the ideas of the 1790s radicals were a long way from being fulfilled even in the mid-nineteenth century. The combination of a narrow religiosity and a concentration on preparing poor children for their inferior role in society ensured that Payne and Wollstonecraft and Rousseau were, not for the last time, being processed in the guts of the mega-machine.

It was Robert Owen who gave hope that the new industrial culture might be able to educate its children humanely. At New Lanark in 1816 the children of his employees in the mills had ten or more teachers between 300 of them, and evening activities, supervised by teachers, were available. Punishments and rewards were out, and lessons were to be 'conveyed in as pleasant and agreeable a manner as can be devised'. This included, as well as the traditional three Rs, sewing, natural history, geography, history, and singing and dancing.

The most influential aspects of Owen's work were the infant school and his linked belief that the environmental conditions around the child were crucial in his or her development. His belief in the possibility of a rational, humane society was stated in *A New View of Society*: 'any general character, from the best to the worst, from the most ignorant to the most enlightened, may be given to any community, even to the world at large'. This optimism, for society and for education, led to the founding of various infant school societies from 1824 onwards. This allowed in the influence of Pestalozzi and other European writers, and led to the kindergarten movement of later in the century.

So were the poor children of mid-nineteenth century England rescued from educational cynicism by a progressive wave of Owenite (or any other) idealism? Joseph Kay, in 1838, reported schoolteachers as 'actually *demoralising* the children'. In 1858 an HMI (Her Majesty's Inspector) reported that 'he knew schools in which he could estimate a pupil's length of stay by the stupidity impressed upon his countenance'.

The government had been putting money into the voluntary schools since 1833 and had contributed to what maintenance of standards did occur by its use of inspectors and, from the 1840s, by putting some resources into teacher-training and incentives. By 1860 there existed a whole system, state-supported and inspected, which in all respects — curriculum, length of school life per pupil, attendance rates and cultural and social objectives — was vastly inferior to that enjoyed by the middle and upper classes. 'Two nations' in education in particular as much as in general.

The lower end of the 'system' of education for the poor consisted of the workhouse schools, ragged schools, and industrial and reformatory schools. Paupers' children were to be educated in the workhouse school, which could be a school shared by several workhouses. Many local boards of Poor Law Guardians felt that paupers' children should have no public money spent on them, and grudgingly provided only nominal teaching. In 1847 an inspection found that twenty-five of forty workhouse teachers in the north of England were themselves paupers, most of them 'grossly incompetent, cannot write, or spell, or ask a question in the proper manner'. Workhouses were widely believed to be extremely bad places for children to be, but they stayed there in large numbers until the end of the century. The mega-machine required the threat of punishment, represented by the workhouse, hanging over the mass of the people as a major weapon of social control, and society's willingness to have children stay there, educated there, is a stark counterpoint to the high ideals to which lip-service was continually paid.

'Ragged schools' began in the 1840s. They were largely provided by the Ragged Schools Union, one of Lord Shaftesbury's causes, and their main purpose was Christian missionary work among destitute and vagrant children. This often involved feeding and lodging the children, of whom there were 25,000 in Union schools in 1870. Those children who slipped through the fingers of the Ragged Schools Union could, on being convicted of vagrancy, be committed to Industrial Schools where craft and domestic skills were given to boys and girls respectively. Children convicted of other offences and imprisoned could afterwards find themselves committed to reformatory schools.

Major attempts to create a stronger system, with schools provided for whole districts paid for out of the rates, were defeated from the 1820s to the 1860s by religious sectarianism. Congregationalists and other non-conformist groups, led from the 1840s by Edward Baines (fire-breathing editor of the *Leeds Mercury*) and Edward Miall, gloried in the demonstration of muscular religiosity. They insisted on taking hundreds of schools out of the system and refusing government money, declaring that the 'power of voluntary Christian zeal' could cater for all 'Education and Religious Instruction, even for a rising population'. By the time they recanted in 1869, admitting they had been wrong, they have been largely responsible for wasting a quarter of a century in the movement towards a national system of free elementary education.

The major criteria for the authorities, some of whom were alarmed that government spending on elementary schools rose from £125,000 in 1848 to £800,000 in 1861, were efficiency and cheapness. It was to increase the one or the other, or both, that 'Payment by Results' was introduced in 1862. Again the outline of the reform may sound familiar. The authorities wished to restrict the freedom of teachers to wander too far from the safe (politically and socially) areas of reading, writing and arithmetic. They also wanted to use annual tests to enforce standards, and if lower standards led to power spending, so be it. Robert Lowe, the (in today's terms) Education Minister told the House of Commons that he could not promise that the new system would be an economical one, 'and I cannot promise that it will be an efficient one, but I can promise that if it is not cheap it shall be efficient; if it is not efficient it shall be cheap'.

The grant for a school — and therefore the teachers' pay — now depended on attendance figures and results of annual inspections of all children in the three Rs. The result, not surprisingly, was that inspectors had neither the time nor the authority to take more than a cursory look at any educational achievements beyond drill in the basics. Rote learning and a narrowing of an often already unambitious curriculum were inevitable, with children being taught, and repeatedly tested, in whatever would get them through the all-important inspection. Children in smaller schools suffered more than the rest, as they could not gain from the economies of scale available for rote learning to large schools. Children in poorer areas suffered further from the inferior attendance figures resulting from higher levels of illness and from parents requiring children to stay at home to work or babysit.

Over a hundred years later, the horrors of the 'Revised Code' with its 'Payments by Results' are enough to send shivers down the spine of any teacher. It was the reaction of increasing numbers of teachers against 'code despotism', as an ex-inspector called it in 1911, and the passionate pleas of leading educationists, such as Edward Thring's demand that teachers 'strive for the liberty to teach', that laid the foundations for the twentieth century's upsurge in educational idealism. The ecological principle was reasserting itself. The hopes of the idealists of 1800 had been swallowed up, digested and rendered into fertiliser for the Owenite reformers of the 1830s; the meagre successes of the mid-century system, represented by increasing spending on education and a widening curriculum, led to another bite-back by the mega-machine, and this in turn eventually fertilised the ground for twentieth century developments.

It is a pity that a century is just long enough for memories to disappear. If teachers really remembered what happened the last time central government took control of the curriculum, enforced crude 'standards' by the use of tests, and elevated efficiency above quality of teaching, would the last ten educational years have really happened?

Of course I have been looking at educational developments as they affected the vast majority of children. The better off had quite other arrangements, and to understand the present system we need to review at least briefly what happened to education for the middle and upper classes during the nineteenth century.

Sons of those on middling incomes went to the endowed school, the old grammar schools. These changed very little over the period of the industrial revolution, partly for legal reasons. The endowments were charitable bequests made to the school by local worthies over the years. The money had to be spent in the same old ways which meant the classical grammars and literatures and little else. In a major court case in 1805, Leeds Grammar School failed to get permission to start teaching modern languages. It was not until 1840 that schools could legally make whatever changes they saw fit to the curriculum.

Many grammar schools declined enormously over the period of early industrialisation. Manchester Grammar School enrolled 548 pupils from 1770 to 1780 and only 288 pupils from 1800 to 1810 (the population more than doubled in this period). Bristol Grammar School was empty from 1800 to 1810 and from 1829 to 1848. Reform was urgently needed.

Reform often — paradoxically to our ears — meant reverting to the strict, narrow, classical curriculum. Modern and commercial studies had entered many curricula, not unconnected with the fact that special fees were payable for them — which, of course, made them largely unavailable to poor scholars. The aim of reform in most grammar schools was to give back to the school the mantle of respectability which Latin and Greek represented.

When the governors of Bradford Grammar School wanted to revive its flagging fortunes by bringing in a curriculum relevant to locally felt needs, the head engaged them in battle. He demanded that the school be restored 'to a purely classical discipline, in order to raise and elevate its character'. Reform of this kind meant fewer free-place pupils, so either way ordinary people lost out. The more successful the reform of an endowed grammar school, the nearer it got to attaining the status of the 'great schools' — public schools like Eton, Harrow and Rugby. Shrewsbury School, for example, made this transition between 1800 and the 1820s. However successful a public school was in attracting boys, it was extremely unlikely to offer anything other than a narrow curriculum and lots of flogging. There were an amazing number of rebellions at public schools during this period, often caused by a mixture of anger over excessive punishments and confused fascination with the revolutionary ideas in the air.

Generally the grammar and public schools prepared the boys of the middle and upper classes, by means of a bastardised classical education rammed down throats by force, for adult lives in the ancient professions or the cultured idleness of the landowning gentry. The astonishing thing is that with such an education for its leadership Britain's industrial revolution and growth were not completely stymied.

Class divisions widened between middle and upper class boys at school. The 'great schools' cut out the sons of tradesmen and the lower orders as mid-century prosperity increased the supply of rich parents and put a premium on exclusivity. Schools were specifically aimed at a particular class (for example Ardingly, for the low middle class). Lancing School went one better and contained two class divisions, paying different fees and using different halls. Are such tendencies, created by the rise of the brash New Right of the 1830s and 40s, entirely without equivalents today?

By mid-century the middle classes were finding more choice in schooling. 'Proprietary schools', run by limited companies with efficient managements and with clear views of their aims (often denominational or commercial and with a modern curriculum) offered competition to the grammar schools. Science, maths and modern languages were taught in some of these schools, but it was only from the 1860s that serious curricular progess was made, following two major commissions of enquiry.

The Clarendon Commission made massive criticisms of the

nine 'great schools', and the Taunton Commission did the same for endowed, private and proprietary schools. Big changes in curricula and methods were recommended, and Acts of Parliament in 1868 and 1869 made the changes possible.

It was no accident that the 1860s saw major changes in education for all classes. Britain was at the peak of its industrial power (the decline relative to other countries like the USA and Germany, though invisible for a long time, began in the 1870s), the empire was expanding rapidly and was expected to continue to do so, and pressure was growing for social and political reform. Efficiency and control, therefore, were of pressing urgency to educational administrators. It was around this time that the cult of the competitive examination grew quickly to impregnable status. The combination of rapid expansion of a wide range of middle class professions, the widening of the curriculum, heightened concern about standards, and the confident belief that the industrial virtues of competition and mechanisation could be applied to schooling, made an enormous exam system irresistably attractive. Secondary school exams began with the Oxford and Cambridge 'locals' in 1858; the Royal Society of Arts and other organisations were running examinations in 'modern subjects'; the army and the civil service were operating sophisticated entrance exams (the latter failing many candidates); and the public and grammar schools were offering many more places by competitive examination.

While some of the endowed, private, proprietary and public schools were beginning to respond in the 1870s to the demands of the Taunton and Clarendon Commissions, elementary schooling was being affected by the Elementary Education Act of 1870. Again, as with each major change, a precarious balancing act had been necessary between the secular enthusiasts — an enormous head of steam had grown up behind the demands for universal elementary schooling, especially in the industrial cities — and the religious vested interests that ran most of the existing elementary schools.

The 1870 Act allowed the creation of School Boards, which were to be elected locally in all districts where there were not enough places in existing schools: it aimed to fill the gaps in a religiously-based system, rather than create a new one. The new public elementary schools were to be specifically aimed at the children of the poor, the range being from the 'street Arab' to the children of the 'respectable working class'. Over thirty years later a National Union of Teachers pamphlet stated: 'Six million children are in the Public Elementary Schools of England and Wales. They are the children of the workers, to be themselves England's workers a few years hence'.

By 1895 average attendance at 2,500 school board schools was nearly 1.9 million and at about 12,000 voluntary schools, 2.4 million. Almost half of those voluntary schools had been built since the Act of 1870, which was extremely generous to the religious interest in building grants as well as in other matters.

The political and social context of the 1870 Act, and of the school boards it created, was of crucial importance then and for a long time afterwards. There are interesting echoes in our own time. The children to be the objects of the boards' mopping-up operation (attendance was made compulsory only ten years later) were the sons and daughters of a working class who had begun to get the vote in 1867. The Reform Act of that year had enfranchised the skilled workman, and much of the middle class pressure for universal education arose from fear of a working class electorate untamed and untrained in correct attitudes by education. Ironically, there was another side of the same coin; the non-conformist voluntary societies were frantically building schools and expanding their rolls as fast as possible, as they desired to keep children out of the irreligious board schools, where they might learn ungodliness and questioning, revolutionary attitudes.

Neither was the political significance of the state's intervention in education lost on radical political writers and organisers. The Social Democratic Federation, the Fabian Society and some Trade Unionists were soon beginning to establish the idea that not only could the state go a lot further in education, but it could usefully intervene in many other areas of life. And the working men who voted, or even stood as candidates, in school board elections, were provided with much good practice in the use of new electoral rights. The attitudes of the forces of reaction today to progressive Local Education Authorities — how easily the 1980s Conservatives got away with abolishing ILEA — and to ordinary people enjoying real democratic rights in education are very reminiscent of the 1870s.

Literacy rates were a measure of the success of the 1870 Act. By 1870 almost all the easier-to-achieve progress had been made, because most of the remaining illiterates were in areas not served by existing schools. The literacy rates for 1871, 1881, 1891 and

1901 for males and females respectively were 80, 87, 94, 97 per cent and 73, 82, 93, 97 per cent. Clearly women had made greater gains in catching up. The chairman of the Ragged Schools Union reported in 1887 that almost every child coming to their schools could read, because of previous attendance at elementary schools: exactly the opposite of the situation earlier.

At the end of the century, though, there was still a great army of children not registered at school, or rarely actually attending. Around 700,000 children who should have been registered were not, and among those registered the average attendance was only just over 80 per cent. The 'board man' who came round after truants could start the prosecution process, but often magistrates were reluctant to convict or to punish severely. It is difficult to judge the relative importance, in the figures for non-registration and non-attendance, of the unattractiveness of life in school and the attractiveness, or necessity, of staying away, for work or play.

The curriculum in schools, under the Revised Code, had begun to relax. Grants could be earned by children passing examinations in extra subjects, such as geography, history, science and languages, though very few children were put forward in this way in the 1870s: the 'Payment By Results' system had had its effect. The system was gradually undermined and improved: new rules in 1882 greatly softened the impact of the annual inspection and a wider range of subjects was allowable. Even school libraries and savings banks were encouraged. Payment by results finally disappeared, after more gradual improvements, in 1893. By then the best elementary schooling was unrecognisably different from the norm of a generation earlier. In 1876 John Ruskin wrote:*

Commiserate the hapless Board School child, shut out from dreamland and poetry, and prematurely hardened and vulgarised by the pressure of codes and formularies. He spends his years as a tale that is *not* told.

But in 1903 Sidney Webb* wrote that the London School Board had brought about

the change from frowsy, dark, and insanitary rooms, practically destitute of apparatus or playgrounds, in which teachers, themselves

---

*Quoted in Lawrence and Silver, *A Social History of England* (Methuen, London 1973).

mostly untrained, mechanically ground a minimum of the three R's
required by the wooden old code into the heads of their scanty
pupils, to the well-lighted and admirably decorated school buildings
of the present day, with ample educational equipment . . . served
by a staff of trained professional teachers, encouraged to develop
the growing intelligence of their scholars in whatever subjects and
by whatever educational methods they find best.

Meanwhile a new sort of school, the 'higher grade' school, had
evolved gradually and almost accidentally, and by 1900 about
two hundred of these were teaching sciences, technical subjects,
maths and languages. Occasionally a pupil would go on to a
grammar school and even university, but normally the higher
grade schools fed boys (and some girls) into skilled and clerical
jobs. The important point, though, is that the need for a proper
secondary system for ex-elementary pupils was becoming obvious. Technical schools and colleges of various kinds were providing more and more education for young artisans, often examined
by the City and Guilds Institute, created in 1880.

Meanwhile large numbers of the endowed grammar schools,
and most of the other fee-paying schools for middle class children,
had widened their curricula, although the changes were slow.
Secondary schooling for girls had made enormous strides. The
status of women was beginning to be changed by the 1870s,
when the Married Women's Property Acts and Matrimonial
Causes Acts began the slow movement towards legal equality.
Smaller families and higher servants' wages at a time of pressure
on middle class incomes — the 1880s and 90s were economically
difficult times — supported the philosophical and campaigning
work being done. The Women's Education Union was founded
in 1871 and its creature, the Girls' Public Day School Trust,
had thirty-six schools by 1894. There were also eighty endowed
schools for girls by then. Most girls' secondary education was
closely modelled on that given to boys, with the addition of
subjects 'appropriate' to domestic work and women's careers.

In the public schools, the period 1870–1900 saw the rise of
boys' games as the British upper classes' response to the demands
of empire. Imperialism was thought to demand of its young
leaders discipline, authority and team spirit, and large amounts
of hard games-playing was the way to produce men of the right
calibre.

So the twentieth century dawned with the education system

ready for another big change. The urgent need to use secondary education, especially technical and scientific, to improve Britain's position in industrial and imperial competition, led the powers that be to turn their minds to creating a proper secondary system for the lower classes. This coincided with an enormous growth in demand from the consumers — ex-elementary pupils — for secondary education. There was also the administrative need to deal with the competition between the school boards and the new Local Authorities who ran technical schools, and generally to supervise an orderly system of post-elementary schooling.

After a great deal of in-fighting, the 1902 Education Act set up the Local Education Authorities more or less as we know them today. But the arguments before the Act, and its details as passed, reflected the authorities' feeling that, after all, secondary education was not really for ordinary people. Elementary schools were firmly put in their place, the higher-grade work was to be much less ambitious, and secondary schooling was to stay very much in the tradition of the old grammar and public schools. The old class divisions were to be strengthened, not weakened. The mega-machine was nowhere near ready to tolerate the threat of an open, democratic education system based on humanistic ideals.

By the 1920s, the system of secondary education had expanded greatly, based on the traditional grammar school. Some older elementary pupils were going to 'higher elementary schools', which were deliberately designed to be of a lower standard. Another Act, in 1918, had fallen victim to financial cutbacks: new demands for a fair secondary system were being made. Sixty-eight per cent of children in secondary schools had been to public elementary schools, but they were less than 10 per cent of the total: the other 90 per cent got no further. 'Secondary Education for All', a 1922 policy statement of the Labour Party, and the official Hadow Report of 1926, supported by a government pamphlet in 1928, prepared the ground for the next great advance. It was not universally popular: the education committee of the Federation of British Industries had warned against 'creating a large class of persons whose education is unsuitable for the employment which they eventually enter', and a retired school medical officer dismissed the Hadow proposals because of 'The too low educability of many of the children' and 'The compulsory nature of the afterlives of the scholars'.

So the period before World War II was a fascinating mix of

ancient and modern. Many enlightened and active authorities were busily reorganising elementary schools, with 'senior departments' or senior schools, and there was intense debate about whether, or how, the lower orders could, or should, have a secondary education. It took a war to provide the political will to push through the changes, which formed the basis of the present system before the introduction of comprehensive schools.

If we are right to be wary of the mega-machine, we must be careful to spot two sets of things. First, which attitudes have really changed? Do the authorities — political and economic — really act today as if they believe that all 5- to 16-year-olds (let alone 16- to 18-year-olds) have the right to a full educational career based on person-centred ideas rather than the requirements of the machine? Does our society make sure that all children are treated equally? Have we grown out of the automatic assumption that learning must come in those boxes, called subjects, convenient for the use of the mega-machine?

Second, what are the relationships between the requirements of the mega-machine and (a) officially-sponsored educational change, and (b) green educational change?

For what sort of world are the officially-sponsored changes trying to prepare, or mould, children? Which aspects of current practice and of the current system are largely in place because of the demands of the mega-machine of today (or yesterday) or tomorrow?

Is there a perfect match, anyway, between the interests of the mega-machine today, and the official perceptions of those interests?

Which bits of a green educational programme, or green educational practice, can survive despite the mega-machine? Does their survival make them, by definition, trivial? Are there ways of moving radically, in a green direction, which could avoid being destroyed by the mega-machine for long enough to make a serious difference? Can green educational work help children better understand, and therefore avoid, or subvert, the mega-machine? Can this work be fully explored within the official system?

This book, I hope, will help readers begin (no more) the process of understanding and answering these questions.

CHAPTER FOUR
What do we want?

'Teaching green' will mean slightly different things, in detail, to different people: people begin the process of 'greening' for many different reasons, from many different starting points. And it would be inconsistent to insist on a simple 'manifesto': part of the greening process is to abandon the mechanistic approach that produces such things, and to open up to the questioning, exploratory approach, which admits of diversity and assumes organic change in the future.

So what follows in this chapter is to be taken in the round, as a broad statement of principle. For some it may articulate fairly accurately what they have been struggling towards, perhaps in different ways. For some it may just add a little to a set of ideas already well articulated. For others it will provide something to disagree with: the start of a fruitful dialogue. For everyone, I hope, it will be the springboard from which to launch into the next questions — 'Can we have something similar to what we want, now?' and 'Where do we look for pointers to the future?' These questions should be answered by subsequent chapters.

When *Green Teacher* magazine was being launched, I had to write an outline of what it thought it was about. Remarkably few green books had given much space to education. I criticised Jonathon Porritt's *Seeing Green* — one of the best, and certainly one of the most influential books in the greening of our political environment — for the shortness of its education section. But there was one passage that was encouraging. On the point that education must foster values more creative, less destructive, than those of industrialism, he said, 'teaching is a subversive activity. But teachers and parents alike must find some way of organising themselves if holistic education, *education for life on earth*, is to have any significant bearing on the future.'

Some starting assumptions

In 1986 I began *Green Teacher*'s position outline by saying, along the same lines as a couple of paragraphs ago: 'Across the movement, around the world, our understanding of what "green" is, is continuously developing and deepening'. But *Green Teacher* had to begin its work under some starting assumptions: all teachers, of all subjects, will want to help students to develop their understanding of, and their skills in helping with, people's need to:

- Co-operate with and care for the earth;
- Co-operate with and care for each other, across boundaries of *all* kinds;
- Grow as independent, self-reliant, confident individuals, able to fulfil themselves;
- Design and use technologies and lifestyles that support these aims, moving towards a sustainable society;
- Work at new ways of 'doing politics', in the basic sense of controlling their future;
- Take part in the spiritual transformation whose 'shifted paradigms' must underlie all other change.

This list has appeared in about 50,000 leaflets and about 3,000 copies of one Green Teacher or another, with just two individual objections. One man wrote an abusive letter, spluttering apoplectically about the use of the word 'paradigm' and how he and his wife, with x degrees between them, could not understand it, and how dare we use the word 'spiritual' when as a chemistry teacher he could tell us that 'green' was all about environmental science, so what on earth were we playing at? The other simply suggested that perhaps we were being a little optimistic talking about people taking control of their futures. To the charge of optimism I will (almost) always plead guilty.

So, possibly, the list *is* a good starting point. Whether it is in the right order is another matter. It is not meant to be an order of priorities, but it may be an interesting exercise to put it in *your* preferred order, if that is possible. Perhaps I should elaborate on each point.

Caring for the earth

Caring for the earth, co-operating with the earth: for most of us, I would guess, the reason we are here — philosophically speaking — is that we have been influenced by, and we have responded personally to, the growing realisation that we must look after our environmental life-support systems better. 'Spaceship Earth', especially after those heart-stopping pictures taken from space, has been an enormously powerful concept. It is one that children understand very well. Young people respond vigorously in discussions to the idea that we are slowly realising it is *our* earth, and *we* are responsible for it.

Green thinking used to be all gloom and doom: the earth was going to run out or crack up or be totally poisoned within *x* years, and so on. Then various catastrophes did not happen, partly because we *had* changed our ways a little, but mainly because the earth is more resilient than some disaster-merchants had feared. But urgent anxiety for the earth, of a more level-headed kind these days, remains the first concern of green thinking for many of us. Acid rain, the greenhouse effect, damage to the ozone layer, pollution of the rivers and the seas, rainforest destruction: perhaps the catastrophes have only been postponed. It is not surprising that environmentalist education is at the top of the agenda.

The environmentalism goes to different depths with different people. Shallow environmentalism — of the sort which says we must look after the trees and clean up the rivers, or whatever, and leaves it at that — should not get much shrift these days. A much more radical approach is needed, combining *both* the deep-ecological approach, which emphasises the sacredness of all of nature around us, *and* the radical social-ecology approach, which insists that environmental problems are put in their social/political context (who benefits from dirty rivers, which human power structure do we need to tackle?) This is the only approach I would call respectable.

There has been a progression, over the last couple of decades, from learning *about* the environment, through learning *from* the environment, through learning *with* the environment, to (and I know it is dangerous to imply that progress has stopped!) learning *for* the environment.

Initially, there was the traditional nature walk, the lessons about trees, about food chains, which for most of us was as far as it went. And, of course, we do still need to learn about these things sometimes. But it was all very limited.

Then came learning from the environment — using the environment in a more rounded, organic way, as a context from which to learn lots of lessons, both factual and not. This was a big improvement. The discovery that 'the environment' was a great big untapped educational resource certainly made dramatic improvements to many children's schooling in the sixties and seventies.

Learning *with* the environment implies a much more active, intimate relationship. Earth Education is one lovely example. In this, children physically enter the oxygen cycle, or actually live at the level of the mini-beasts. It is one of the most exciting manifestations of the idea of experiential learning: getting in amongst it all!

But, the question has to be asked, what is it all *for*? Why is it important to know about the earth, or to be able to learn from the environment, or to grow as a person through physical experiences with it? Of course, assuming one has in mind that we are teaching for active democracy, the whole point, or at least a significant part of it, is to *do* something about it. It is this sense that we will have to take co-operative action for the earth, that caring is not just a passive enjoyment of the wonders of nature, which makes today's radical environmental education exciting.

Caring for each other

For many of us, co-operating with each other, trying to move away from a competitive ethos to a caring one, is integral to the greening of our lives. For some, it is the prime stimulus in this direction: they grew up in the tradition of left or liberal politics in Britain, in which social justice was the driving force of political beliefs. Growing disillusion with conventional left politics, growing realisation of the needs of the earth, growing disappointment with the poverty of our institutionalised ways of caring, have combined to prompt a greening of their socialism. For others, the urgent need of the human race to do something to ensure peace, to dismantle the nuclear arsenals, has been the motivating force. For still others, the immediate reason for concern was one or other of the barriers mentioned. Racial barriers, sexual barriers, national barriers, social barriers: they all damage people; a society with caring as its central value means, for some of us, first and foremost one that dismantles and discards the barriers that are tolerated, or even encouraged, in traditional conventional society.

For me, it is not respectable to separate caring for the earth from caring for people. The moral imperatives, both for the one and for the other, share the same root. Whether you believe that God made the earth with us on it, or that, in a less traditionally deistic sense, there is a spiritual connection between us and the rest of nature, or that, in a secular sense, it is not rational to try to care for the one without caring for the other because they need each other, does not matter. They go together at whatever level.

It follows that we must help children learn about caring for the earth and about caring for each other in such a way that they are able to integrate the two. The emphasis must sometimes be on the one or theother, but I hope there is agreement on intimate philosophical and practical links between the two. One of the most encouraging developments of recent years has been the way that educators have made links between peace education and environmental education. The book *Education for Peace* (1988), edited by David Hicks of the Centre for Peace Studies at Lancaster, is very well worth a look on this point.

Growing to fulfilment

The idea that growing should be a central concern in education has been around for a long time: as we saw earlier, progressive educators have always emphasised the growth of the child's inner nature. The 'personal growth industry' of the last couple of decades has offered some absurd excesses, often blamed in Britain on creeping Californianism. But it is clear that in the education of most children today, we could do a lot more about the life of Rousseau's 'secret heart'.

Most educational aims are still couched in terms of what things we want children to learn, and what skills we want them to acquire. Growth, of course, can be (and often is) a small by-product of such learning, but education will be very different if growth is set at the centre and not just assumed as an optional extra. There are powerful vested interests in our culture that do not want people to comprehend and strive towards their potential as human beings. It would be extremely inconvenient for the advertising machine, for the bureaucratic machine, for the war machine, and for all the other components of the mega-machine.

The humanistic psychologists of whom Carl Rogers is the best known (see his book *Freedom to Learn*, 1983), have again in the last thirty years been emphasising the absolute importance of encouraging young people to explore themselves, to enjoy the process of self-realisation. As we take in and apply these messages, the narrow, confined, mechanical schooling of their parents and grandparents — that's us — will seem more and more quaint as time goes on. We want to green education in such a way that young people feel more able to think and act independently, with more confidence, proud of their self-reliance and able to co-operate with others. To the extent that we succeed in this, we will have enabled them to enjoy life as it is now and prepared them for life with the mega-machine — or, ideally, after it.

Appropriate technology

Technology choice is something that traditionally we have taught as being outside the province of ordinary people: the experts or the leaders would deliver the technology and we would just work it or enjoy it. Alternative Technology has developed in the last few decades as a response to the realisation that conventional ways of using technology ignored many important non-financial, non-technical criteria. It has been a positive movement that has shown that it is possible to provide for human needs with much less damage to resources and to our ecosystem.

For most people working in Alternative Technology, it has many other connotations. On the same lines as my point about not separating care for people from care for the earth, alternative technology is associated with a move away from materialism towards increased care for personal relationships, away from individualism towards collective, co-operative ways of organising our lives, away from compartmentalisation of issues towards holism. The aim is sustainability for our lives on earth, and alternative technology has for many people been the route by which they came to deeper understandings of what that means — in both practical hardware or process and in attitudes.

Educators helping children and students design and use sustainable technologies clearly involves several areas of the school curriculum: Science, CDT (Craft, Design, Technology), and Humanities at the least. From my experience as an Education Officer at the Centre for Alternative Technology, I can report that a very large, and increasing, number of schoolteachers are introducing their pupils to alternative technology. How deep the introduction goes — it can be just at the technical level, though that is at least a start — is another question. But it is encouraging that, often, the main reason the Centre has not provided more courses for school and college students, and inservice training courses for teachers, is that it has been more or less full: in 1988 and 1989 we ran over seventy different residential courses for these groups, in addition to other categories of course. It is on these residential courses, and on similar ones run by LEAs, that students relax, get below the surface of the subject, and integrate their technological education with their concern for people and planet.

There are a number of CDT teachers working hard to green their subject, and we have a contribution from one of the most active ones, Colin Mulberg, in the next chapter. Another organis-ation doing valuable work in this area is the Intermediate Tech-nology Development Group (IT). Most of their efforts go into researching and introducing productivity-raising intermediate technology in Third World countries, but they have in the last couple of years begun to run a serious education service too. A publication for CDT teachers due out in late 1989, to which a group of us from all around the country contributed ideas and materials, should be extremely helpful. More about IT, too, later.

Doing politics

Working at new ways of doing politics is potentially the most subversive item on our list. It is still a newsworthy event for the local press when a school holds a mock election, even more so when a sixth-form conference is organised in the form of a meet-ing of the United Nations General Assembly.

These can be worthwhile educational activities, given a range of qualifications about the supposed realism of the event (it is impossible to convey to children, or for them to learn fully for themselves, the crassness and corruption inherent in conven-tional politicking), about the relations between children and teachers during the event (I have been in a school where the head imposed severe constraints on which parties pupils could choose to represent and where miseducation, via falsification and idealisation of the process, seemed to outweigh any positive gains), and about the *context* in which they occur (too often they are isolated events, unconnected with both the regular curricu-lum and the politics of the school).

But if such events are the main examples given when a school tells you it has a proper programme of political education, smell a rat. Most teachers are brought up in a hierarchical, bureaucratic education system; they are not often closely exposed to the progressive end of even the conventional political spectrum in their own lives; and they are untrained in participatory methods of helping their pupils to experience democracy in education. It is not surprising, then, that political education, apart from some shining examples, is desultory at best.

With the screws holding down schools and teachers having been tightened during the Thatcher years, it is a difficult time for any political education that goes beyond the attempt to train for acquiescent, superficial citizenship. But green politics (not *necessarily* anything to do with the Green Party) is about devolution of power, about openness and egalitarianism, about the engagement of the whole person in the whole process, and about applying ecological principles of diversity and respect for life to the *process* of how we conduct our affairs.

It is not good enough to green a part of the curriculum content, or even teaching methods too, and ignore the vital lessons for life learned via the hidden curriculum of how the politics of the school are conducted. We know from past experience that it is possible for headteachers to relinquish some of their control, allowing young people to take responsibility for important areas of their lives and learn about politics by experience.

Children who have grown up being encouraged to question and discuss, encouraged to exercise their rights to engage in the political process — not just as occasional election fodder but as an organic part of normal life — are dangerous children. They can be — sometimes are — given a hard time by authority. But that can be a useful learning experience if they have proper support, to bind the wounds and raise the spirits. We need such children, and a major part of 'what we want' is an education in which they can flourish.

Spiritual transformation

The 'spiritual transformation' that is the last of our 'starting assumptions' can occasionally be a little threatening, as we saw with my apoplectic correspondent. It is true that one of the main barriers between the more fervently spiritual citizens of the 'new age' and the rest of humanity is the language they use. But, at the least, it is also difficult to explore recent green thinking about the current stage of our civilisation's history without acknowledging that many people are reaffirming some important spiritual truths buried during the centuries of the mega-machine's growth, and/or discovering new spiritual truths.

Our civilisation has suppressed truths about the human being's inner life, denied the importance of the non-material, and peddled a perverted spirituality, in the form of conventional religion, as a major weapon against the growth of the free, spiritually-connected, whole citizen. The paradigm — the way of thinking, the world view — that has sustained western scientistic materialistic civilisation is creaking at the seams. The scientific bases of its materialist certainties are being eroded by twentieth century physics, the cultural pillars that have supported it, such as that men must dominate nature and women, are being exposed as false, and its assumption of unlimited material progress is becoming disreputable.

The works of Fritjof Capra and Charlene Spretnak are probably the best entry to recent developments. Capra's *The Turning Point* is a wonderful overview of a civilisation in crisis and a convincing demonstration of the need to build on the knowledge and skills we already have available to us in going on to the next stage, beyond the turning point. Spretnak has shown, in *The Spiritual Dimension of Green Politics* (originally a Schumacher lecture in the USA) that green politics, out there in the real world, need the spiritual dimension if they are to be fully informed, if they are to reach deep into people, and ultimately if they are going to work.

Charlene Spretnak presents at the end of her book the 'Ten key values of the American green movement', quoted in Part Two below. The questions by which these values are presented add up to a basis for a whole year of creative discussion with young people. 'Values education' has been around for some years and it can be a liberating feature of an otherwise sterile curriculum. What we want for our children is that they are able to develop their values in a context of reverence for the earth, and for all of life, in a context that enables them to deal with their material environment *and* to make contact with the non-material realities.

I believe that, working from our six starting assumptions, we can satisfy all the other demands on green education. These 'other demands' do, however, need to be looked at.

Smallschooling, minischooling, flexischooling . . .

One major demand in recent years, and there has been an active, articulate lobby with this as its slogan, is for 'human scale' education. Small really is usually more beautiful, and in education, which ultimately rests on human relationships, giantism causes great problems. Big systems, big schools, are difficult places in which to foster the intimate, confidence-building relationships without which green education is impossible.

The Human Scale Education Movement was founded in 1985, in response to the widespread feeling that the system of education in the UK had lost its way and was in need of reform on human scale principles. More and more parents, teachers and educationists felt that running schools like factories with pupils as their products was not the way to educate children. They saw the need to develop learning systems on a human scale, in which children were regarded as individuals. Their first national conference was held in Oxford in 1987 and this proved to be a seminal meeting: I have several times been engaged in conversation by people who began by referring to that conference or the resolution that came out of it.

The 1987 conference reaffirmed the aims of the Human Scale Education Movement:

A. The reform of large schools through the introduction of human scale structure within them, e.g. minischools.

B. The rescue of small schools from the threat of closure through falling rolls.

C. The restoration of small schools to communities by founding new ones, to be funded in the maintained system.

In particular, the movement:

1. Welcomes the efforts of those in schools and LEAs who are working to develop education along human-scale lines.

2. Will support those efforts by exchanging information and ideas and encouraging new initiatives.

3. Urges the government to publicise its proposals for a New Education Act more effectively and allow realistic time for consultation, making resources available for this alternative process.

4. Urges LEAs to consider their policies for cooperation and contact with all parents, including those educating their children otherwise.

5. Urges the government to include in the New Act provisions for the support of parents, teachers and the local community to start new schools or to support existing independent schools, provided they meet certain conditions such as:
- they are non-fee-paying;
- they have open access;
- they are accountable to the local community and the funding authority.

This would mean that such schools would receive the same per capita funding as any other maintained school, along the lines of the Danish and Dutch systems.

6. As there is some evidence that small schools are not less effective than large schools, we urge the government to put no restriction on the minimum size of schools.

Philip Toogood of the Human Scale Education Movement is head of Dame Catherine's, a small school in Derbyshire that was rescued from closure (the LEA were about to close it down as too small and a local group got together and organised its reopening for the following day!). He was the architect of 'minischooling', which involves creating human-scale units, with real autonomy, within the giant institution. His book *Minischooling* describes the scheme fully, and fascinatingly. In one place in England minischooling was so successful that the grateful but unimaginative governors subsequently felt that their school's problems — which had been great — were now solved, and they could revert to conventional ways. Sometimes you just cannot win.

A third scheme in the Human Scale list of policy goals is flexischooling, the idea that children should, flexibly, alternate between learning in and out of school. Several thousand children — estimates go up to 10,000 — are currently being educated 'otherwise', i.e. at home. The 'otherwise' comes from the phrase in the 1944 Education Act, which obliged parents to see that their children received an education, either at school 'or otherwise'. Homeschoolers are not typically against schools in principle, it's just that, for the time being, it seems that a particular child's needs are better catered for out of school. Many homeschoolers, moreover, strongly dislike having to choose between the two extremes: in or out of school all the time. This is where the idea of flexischooling comes in.

The term flexischooling first emerged in discussions between Roland Meighan of the Department of Education at Birmingham University, and John Holt, the US educationist whose book *How Children Fail* became one of the best-known condemnations of conventional schooling. Meighan's book *Flexischooling* is a superb outline of the arguments and dreams that flexischooling inspires.

Flexischooling may seem outlandish, but it becomes more and more commonsensical the more one remembers that education can and does go on in many, varied locations:

- Parents need not be part of the problem of education, they can be active, creative partners, with schools, in the solution.

- Children can learn without a teacher present: distance-learning today is a fast-growing field, with over a hundred years' experience in the Worldwide Education Service alone.

- Teaching does not equal instructing: the facilitation of learning is what we want, and it can be done in an infinite number of places, by an almost infinite number of people, in an almost infinite number of ways.

- The resources for increasing flexibility today are mind-bogglingly plentiful: TV, video, computers, computer networks, audio tapes.

Conventional schooling may be too slow to change, to adapt to the demands for flexibility arising both from the pace of change in the real world outside and from the rising demands of parents and children. The experience of those inside the system trying to introduce radical change is that it is often extremely difficult: enormous vested interests can be very obstructive.

But the case for a wider choice is so clear, and the bankruptcy of conventional ideas so obvious, that I would not be at all surprised — and certainly would not be unhappy — to see great progress being made quite soon towards widespread flexischooling. Dame Catherine's School has already shown the way: let's hope it's not long before large numbers of others follow.

Lesson content

'What do we want?' often means what do we want our children to learn *about*? This is clearly a question about content of lessons. The conventional way for a teacher to approach an educational activity with children is to formulate a list of aims and objectives, then to adopt a method of achieving the aims and objectives. Typically the aims and objectives are the content which it is hoped to deliver: knowledge gained, skills learned or practised, values examined or whatever. Then the 'method' is the means of delivery of the content.

As a way of describing most activities that happen in schools, this is accurate. Whether or not it is education is another matter. Before we go any further, I must admit a major problem. I am going to try to indicate (in a small space it cannot be much more) that this approach is philosophically and practically flawed as a way of doing green education, because it is based on a false dualism, or separation. The problem is the Catch–22 that having been trained in a dualistic system, having succeeded with Cartesian ways of thinking, I find it difficult to make the jump to where I know we ought to be. My mindset was fixed — almost — a long time ago. It makes for imprecise writing and a frustrating lack of exact formulae: the desire for precision and formulae, of course, is frustrating precisely because of the paradigm we're trying to struggle out of. This could get worse if we don't just relax and accept a move in the right direction. . . .

Content and method exist, of course, separately, in most educational activities, in the sense that we can usually see them and deal with them in discussion, separately. What we want to move towards, is learning being carried on by self-directed students using the teacher as a consultant and facilitator — content and method 'subsumed' into a *process*. The process itself would be the important thing. This is education experienced as investigation, discussion, discovery and creation, with the mechanistic ideas of 'what's the content?' and 'what's the method?' becoming redundant.

All this is a bit abstract and perhaps difficult to pin down. But the best primary teaching practice is sometimes like this already, and we have all had a thousand experiences of it in our adult lives. The teacher who has so organised his/her classroom, and so inspired the children, that an active investigatory or discovery or creative process takes hold, can neither predict exactly what any child will learn, nor have close control over the methods of learning. It is rarely totally open-ended of course, nor should it necessarily be so, but once the process has started it has a life of its own in each child that far transcends in quality anything to be gained from the dualistic approach.

Setting up the process, of course, is a teaching technique, but is a lot further back, less constricting, than more formal techniques. And because it allows for individual needs and maximises learner freedom, it is green teaching. Similarly, as adults we are taken into a self-directed process when something — a question we just have to find the answer to, a technical problem we become engrossed in solving, the artistic challenge of understanding a difficult play or piece of music — absorbs our total attention. We learn far more, and more effectively, than we could be taught in the content and method manner.

For everyday purposes, however, most of the time, most teachers have to work within constraints that make the conventional approach reasonable: so in our present, transitional age we must talk about contents and methods of 'teaching green'.

So what will the content be? I do not think I should answer that question, except to point to the practical implications of the six assumptions discussed earlier. The national curriculum in Britain — insofar as schools stick to it — is going to narrow the range of what some 5- to 16-year-olds learn. But it will still be possible to demand that all the content you can generate, from a brainstorm based on the assumptions, be included. The checklist section should help with details.

And methods? Clearly the teacher must evolve from the central authority figure to being the sort of facilitator described earlier. The green teacher does not operate only as a scene-setter and consultant, however: there are much more active roles on other occasions. In fact, active learning, the collaboration of teacher and learner sparking off educational processes through a series of activities, as opposed to book learning exercises, has been at the centre of some of our most exciting curriculum development work, like World Studies and Global Education, which are mentioned in the next chapter. There are lots of jargon phrases (the experience-centred curriculum is a good one!) but the common factor is the engagement of the students in an active process.

At the same time as process takes over from content and method, *context* becomes a crucial concept. As a simple example, there is not a lot of point, educationally, in learning simply that one makes a solar panel (to take a random example) in a particular, technical way. It becomes important if one has set one's learning about solar power in the context of renewable energy. Why bother with renewable energy? What are the implications of using it? With what other concerns does it connect? In another area of the curriculum, a historical fact is not a lot of use except insofar as it helps us understand a system of connected facts and figures, and through them, something of importance for today and tomorrow.

So pertinent questions about a particular child's learning can centre on *what* is being learned, and *how*, in the conventional way, but you will find out a lot more of importance if you pursue questions about process and context. So we can add a further answer to the question 'What do we want?': lots more emphasis on process, and large helpings of contextualisation!

School and community

To expand our idea of what the curriculum will look like, we should also be demanding new relationships between schools and their communities. What sort of links are normal now, and in what directions would we like to go?

Traditionally the headteacher has spent a lot of time keeping the school and community apart: acting as a buffer when 'interfering' people showed an interest in entering on the hallowed ground. Once, as a keen young(ish) head of department in a 'Community High School', I was asked by a pupil's mother if she could join in on my History 'O' level class. So I went along to the head: this was the first such request in the brand-new school, it was an exciting opportunity.

'Christ, how can we get out of this one?' was his immediate reaction. Deflation. Disillusion. Disappointment. Neither she nor any other adult joined a class in that school.

At the other end of the scale there are schools that welcome members of the community, whose students go out and back and forth purposefully and fruitfully.

There are different levels at which the community–school relationship is important. The community around a school, first, is a rich resource. There are more sources of information and ideas among the people of the community, at home and at work, than the teachers could ever provide inside the school buildings.

The community, second, can provide a range of long-term learning experiences impossible in the school. 'City as School' is the most exciting example, detailed below, but in Britain today some of the more imaginative 'work experience' schemes have shown the way.

Third, and most importantly, it is only via organic links between community and school-based learning that children and students can contextualise their learning: 'What is it all *for*? How is it connected with "real life"? If I'm "learning green" so as, partly, to be able to change the world,' (and you are) 'which bits do I want to think about changing now, and how can I operate as an active democrat *now*?'

One scheme, in New York City, takes this to the extreme. Students at 'City as School' spend their time — 25 to 32 hours per week — at a series of 'learning experience centres'. These are organisations of a business, cultural or civic nature: examples are *Art in America* magazine, New York City Opera, New York Botanical Gardens, hospitals and fashion houses. The student attends one or a series of centres during any given month. There is a central staff, devising and monitoring students' experiences, so that each student's two-year course is uniquely suited to his/her needs.

The scheme is a success from the point of view of the authorities — it has expanded onto new sites and gained a major national curriculum award. And the students — who in the main were not successful in mainstream schooling — make remarkable progress, very often going on to college when that had previously seemed impossible. I found these students' comments most revealing:

I have been at this school for two and a half years . . . I've tutored, taught, and campaigned. I've pottered, printed, and sewn. I've been through the worst of the best and the best of the worst. But, every decision I made — well, almost every one — was on my own, and I took the consequences. That's what we all have done.

SHERRY SANTOS

I never thought I'd be going to college, but now that I've actually finished high school I have a better understanding of what college can be like. I learned how to work and study on my own while I was at CAS. . . . Unlike many high school grads, I've had a chance to experience what it's like in the world of working people.

TANYA BISHOP

The key to CAS [City as School] is responsibility. You have to go in thinking positively about doing a good job at the resources you have chosen, and go when you're supposed to be there. I have worked from 9.00 in the morning until 9.30 at night. . . . For the most part, I attended regularly, but much of the time it wasn't easy. CAS wants a person who 'isn't afraid to try something new' and go out and do real work — and a good job.

GREG MURRAY

City as School feeds students who are hungry to find out what life is all about. Not only does CAS supply students with a taste of responsibility and accomplishment, it also fills them with pride, confidence, and dignity.

KIM LYONS

So, 'what do we want?' includes a substantial improvement in the quantity and quality of school–community links.

Qualification: this section should not be taken to mean that I feel that there is no place for 'protecting' in-school learning from the outside world. We can all think of examples, but here are two important ones. First, there are some educational experiences that depend utterly on an intimacy, a private act of trust between teacher and learner, and for which the protected space is vital. It could be an exploration of emotional geography in a drama session, or a more mundane, but just as vulnerable, first attempt at some new curricular project, or whatever. Protection, privacy, separateness behind the school walls, may be appropriate.

Secondly, one of the jobs of the school is to introduce children to universal ideas, ideals and culture, beyond the immediate community, beyond the national or even the continental community. There is a danger of community-rooted education allowing the parochial and specific to edge out the universal: what we want, as in all good ecosystems, is diversity and balance!

School and parents

Parents, of course, are the crucial members of the community, and what we want must include a new relationship between parents and school. I once offered my services — as a listener to children reading, or whatever — to my child's infant school headteacher. 'Oh no,' was the reply, 'if we have one parent in, others will want to come, and we *are* next to a council estate'.

That may be extreme (why have so many extremely sad things happened to me? It's enough to make one bitter and twisted . . .) but it points up the fact that parents are grossly undervalued as resources.

What we want includes a redefinition of the relationship of the job of parent with the job of school teacher in the joint enterprise of education. This involves new ways of relating to each other. It is not good enough to run arm's-length PTAs and read reports and attend open days and vote for parent–governors occasionally. This is the dessicated, pseudo-participatory Bakerite approach. What we want includes parents making active, effective contributions to curriculum discussions and decisions on extra-curricular use of resources. It includes parents acting in the curriculum, in and out of school, and it includes substantial moves towards freedom of movement for all individual children, so that those who need it can alternate the location of their learning base from home to school and back again: flexischooling.

So, what we want amounts to quite a lot: a curriculum based on green values; education at a human scale; a rethinking of 'content and method'; large moves towards participatory, process-based learning; and radical changes in the relationship of schools with their communities, and with their parents. One danger with generating a long list of ambitious demands, sometimes, is that it can be over-facing: 'Oh, we'll never get anywhere near that lot. . .'. What follows, though, should be encouraging: the different elements of teaching green are around already, to varying degrees. It *is* possible to be optimistic!

PART TWO
TEACHING GREEN IN PRACTICE

Introduction

The following collection of items, some pieces about one element or another of teaching green, others examples of teaching materials, should do several things. It will encourage the parent who finds it difficult, as an 'outsider', to put a finger on what we mean when we talk about green teaching. (It will be comforting, I hope, to find that much of the background work, much of the thinking and development of materials, has already been done, and is just waiting for teachers to pick it up.) It will provide a gold-mine of ideas to mull over for practising teachers who wish to move in a green direction: perhaps even something for next week's lessons! And it may spark off some thoughts in those who are just beginning to be interested — parents and teachers — about having a further look.

The items are grouped according to a sort of logic. The problem with this is that it is bound to contradict what I said earlier about the holistic approach, about the integrated nature of our ideal green education. Still, no doubt you will make your own connections. I just hope that the grouping I have used is more helpful than not, and I suggest that, having had a first look-through, you ignore it!

Acknowledgement details: full details of each non-*Green Teacher* source are given in 'Resources'. I am very grateful to all those sources for permission to reprint here. *Green Teacher* references are to issue numbers: 'Resources' has information about back-numbers and offprints.

1: People and planet

Earthrights

The terms environmental education and development education may not be familiar. *Earthrights — Education as if the Planet Really Mattered* is a wonderful book for teachers, arising out of the 'Global Impact' project at the Centre for Global Education at York University. Before going on to inspire and assist teachers who want to explore the integration of these two curricular areas, it gives an outline of each. Environmental education has developed from an early, narrow focus on the local environment, usually biology-based, to a holistic, 'bio-political' approach. In environmental education today we increasingly find:

- a recognition that the local environment is caught up in the global ecosystem;

- an awareness that human and natural systems interact in myriad ways and that there is no part of human activity which does not have a bearing on the environment and vice versa;

- a dawning acknowledgement of how much we can learn from other cultures and, perhaps especially, indigenous peoples, about how to relate to the environment;

- an emphasis on the development of environment-friendly values, attitudes and skills (including, very importantly, those skills appropriate to influencing public opinion and political decision-making).

[From *Earthrights — Education as if the Planet Really Mattered*, by Sue Grey, Graham Pike and David Selby]

Development education, too, has moved on in the last twenty years. After early work that focused on problems experienced by Third World countries, current practice in the classroom increasingly includes these insights.

- To understand the level of development in a particular country,

74

the impact of global economic and political systems has also to be studied.

- Development education is about understanding development processes within and between all countries, rich and poor.
- What is appropriate development in one context is not necessarily appropriate in another.
- Those in the West have much to learn from non-Western perspectives on development.
- The 'Third World' is not just a term to describe economically poor nations, but also encompasses areas and groups that have been marginalised by the workings of economic and political systems (e.g. women, the aged, the homeless, the unemployed, ethnic minorities, indigenous peoples, and poor, remote or uninfluential parts of wealthy countries).

[From *Earthrights* — *Education as if the Plant Really Mattered*]

Global Education also embraces human rights education and peace education, each of which also has a narrow focus and a broad focus. The links that we see when we look at the broad focus of each of these 'four educations' make them, as *Earthrights* put it, 'complementary, interdependent, and mutually illuminating'.

Global impact

The Global Impact survey (1986–87), covering over 800 primary and secondary teachers in twenty-one randomly selected LEAs, produced extremely interesting results — some encouraging, some less so, but all useful for all of us demanding more 'teaching green'.

Seventy-five per cent of teachers think that 'developing an understanding that the world is an interrelated, interdependent system of lands and peoples' is very important or crucial in the promotion of a global perspective in education.

Forty-six per cent of teachers indicated that their school had policies or guidelines which feature environmental education.

Sixty-nine per cent of teachers think that environmental and development education are relevant to their subject areas.

Variations in teaching/learning styles used when dealing with development/environmental issues

	Primary	Secondary	Science	English, languages	Humanities	Art, music, PE, design
% adopting personal focus	84	63	57	80	60	60
% using role play fairly or very frequently	14	22	4	38	23	15
% using simulations fairly or very frequently	12	24	10	35	27	23
%using co-operative learning fairly or very frequently	71	41	30	53	40	54

Variation in the percentage of teachers dealing with particular themes

	Primary	Secondary	Science	English, languages	Humanities	Art, music, PE, design
Aid	30	20	6	20	40	11
Arms trade	2	7	1	6	12	1
Endangered species	47	19	38	21	13	7
Energy	46	46	72	11	54	26
Futures	10	25	12	37	22	22
Habitat conservation	40	40	58	19	36	16
Human rights	15	31	8	44	46	11
Interdependence	24	22	17	10	41	11
Multicultural issues	30	30	8	39	45	19
North/south conflict	3	20	4	7	49	–
Other lands and peoples	65	32	14	26	62	22
Peace issues	7	14	2	25	23	1
Pollution	50	50	73	33	55	23
Urban issues	18	31	10	24	60	12
Work	48	30	15	44	46	20

[Global Impact report summary, Sue Greig]

Sixty-seven per cent of teachers think that the political aspects of development and environmental education are *not* too controversial to be dealt with in the classroom.

Eighty-eight per cent of primary and secondary school teachers think that the children they teach are *not* too young to develop a global awareness or empathy with people from other lands and cultures.

Seventy-eight per cent of primary and secondary school teachers think that development and environmental education are central to achieving an understanding of, and active participation in the world today.

Sixty-five per cent of primary and secondary teachers would welcome in-service training on ways of incorporating develoment and environmental issues into their teaching.

[From *Earthrights — Education as if the Planet Really Mattered*]

Global Teacher, Global Learner

The team who produced *Earthrights* went on to produce in 1988 *Global Teacher, Global Leader*, the 'definitive handbook' for teachers who want to adopt the approach to teaching and learning of Global Education (or you may have come across the term World Studies: they usually mean the same thing). It is very much a book for teachers, and is the prime source for any school or department wishing to go in this direction. But we can all gain a lot of encouragement from the hundreds of activities suggested (all of which are actually done, somewhere, with real students and real teachers!) One example, a good way into the concept of interdependence of global issues, is 'Woolly Thinking':

Woolly Thinking

Resources

For a class of thirty students: 10 sheets of sugar paper, 10 sets of labels (3 per set and each set of a different colour), 30 pins, scrap paper and 10 balls of wool of colours to match the labels.

A large open space in the classroom is required so that the following arrangement is possible:

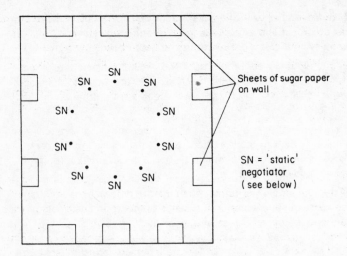

The ten chosen topics should be written up at the top of the sugar paper, one on each sheet. Topics could be: The Arms Race, Environmental Pollution, Unemployment, 'Third World' Underdevelopment, Terrorism/Freedom Fighting, Human Rights Violations, Nationalism, Natural Resource Depletion, Malnutrition, Urbanisation. The topics should also be written on the sets of labels.

Procedure

Students choose one of the ten topics by standing next to a particular sheet of sugar paper. There should be no more than three students per group. Each student should wear a label identifying her as representing that particular topic. Groups first brainstorm the issues surrounding their topic using the scrap paper provided (8 minutes). They then appoint a 'static' negotiator and two 'mobile' negotiators. The 'static' negotiators should take up position in a circle and tie the ends of their balls of wool around their waists. Their role is to stay in one position but to join in negotiations with any of the 'mobile' negotiators of the nine other groups. The role of the 'mobile' negotiator is to go out and negotiate connections, links or relationships between topics. Each time a connection between two topics has been discussed and agreed, the two balls of wool are passed across the circle and looped around the waists of the 'static' negotiators of the two groups concerned.

It is important that the wool is kept taut and that the ball is brought back to the 'static' negotiator from whom it started each time. It is also very important that the thinking behind each agreement is recorded by 'mobile' negotiators of both groups on their respective sheets of sugar paper. As the activity continues, a spider's web of connections between the 10 issues will be produced; the web will probably be so closely woven that 'mobile' negotiators will have to crawl underneath in pursuit of their task.

Potential

The web of different coloured wools offers a potent visual symbol of the interlocking/systemic nature of contemporary global issues. Throughout the discussion it is helpful to keep the web intact. This can be done by asking 'static' negotiators to sit down where they have been standing. Class members can be encouraged to describe the negotiations in which they were involved and to reflect upon the connections made during the activity. Discussion of the absence of connections can also be very productive. **Woolly Thinking** is an ideal unit for exploring relationships between topics on which students have already undertaken some background work.

Variations

The topics used are, of course, open to considerable variation. Upper primary and lower secondary teachers have used **Woolly Thinking** to illustrate the food web and other types of ecological interdependence. It can also be used to illustrate local community interdependencies and the relationships between characters in stories or novels.

Primary/Secondary, 25 minutes.

Source

Centre for Global Education.
[From *Global Teacher, Global Learner*, by Graham Pike and David Selby]

Peace Education

Peace Education emerged, in the late 1970s, from two much older traditions and one of a generation or so ago. The older ones are those of libertarian education and of personal growth education, both of which grew in the twentieth century but have roots going much further back (Rousseau again!). The later one is education for international understanding which largely grew out of personal lessons learnt in this century's World Wars.

By the 1970s peace researchers in universities were developing more sophisticated ideas of violence — and therefore of peace — than simply direct violence, like fighting. Indirect, structural violence can be just as destructive, and while we need the 'negative peace' which we get from the absence of war, we also need the 'positive peace' of absence from structural violence, if we are to live fulfilled lives. Figure 1 is a good discussion starter.

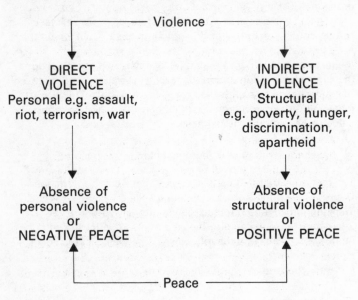

Figure 1: Defining peace. From Hicks, David (ed.), Education for Peace.

Education for peace

The tasks for the 1990s in peace education derive from the multifacetedness of the crises facing humankind, and the interrelatedness of our responses to them. *Education for Peace* suggests ten pointers to future developments in the world studies field:

1. *World studies* — there will be an increasing interest in world studies programmes, and projects such as *World Studies 8–13*, as providing a practical and clear embodiment of education for peace principles in action.
2. *Anti-racism* — there will be increasing recognition that peace education must be anti-racist in its stance, but also a realisation that anti-racism can learn from the insights of peace education.
3. *Gender* — peace education practitioners will play their part in developing anti-sexist curricula and equal opportunities for girls and women, and in challenging male socialisation into patterns of violence.
4. *Human rights* — there will be increasing emphasis on teaching and learning about justice, rights, and responsibilities, in both local, national, and international contexts.
5. *Media* — increasing attention will be paid to the role of the media in influencing children's attitudes towards violence as well as affecting the formation of their views of the world.
6. *World development* — there will be a continued emphasis on teaching about North-South issues and increasing links with those involved in development education and with Development Education Centres.
7. *Controversy* — more consideration will be given to clarifying the characteristics of indoctrination and to the specific professional and ethical responsibilities of teachers when teaching about controversial issues.
8. *International links* — there will be increasing links with peace and global education initiatives, especially with Europe, the USA, Australia, and Canada.
9. *National curriculum* — careful attention will be given to the ways in which specific subject areas can contribute to an understanding of issues to do with peace and conflict as well as to the ways in which they can benefit from peace education methodology.
10 *Process* — the process of person-centred education and active learning will be continually reaffirmed, and particular attention will be given in this respect to classroom management and school organisation.

[From *Education for Peace*, edited by David Hicks]

Peace education, more than any other, emphasises process alongside, or above, content. The 'summary of objectives' in Figure 2 indicates the priorities.

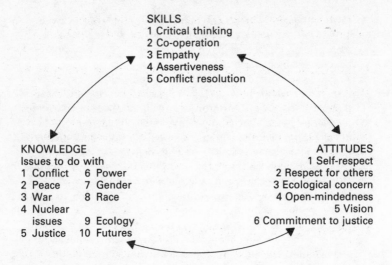

SKILLS
1 Critical thinking
2 Co-operation
3 Empathy
4 Assertiveness
5 Conflict resolution

KNOWLEDGE
Issues to do with
1 Conflict   6 Power
2 Peace   7 Gender
3 War   8 Race
4 Nuclear
  issues   9 Ecology
5 Justice   10 Futures

ATTITUDES
1 Self-respect
2 Respect for others
3 Ecological concern
4 Open-mindedness
5 Vision
6 Commitment to justice

Figure 2: A visual summary of objectives. From Hicks, David (ed.),
Education for Peace.

Futures

Futures education — which aims to enable children to be confident and creative about the sort of future they want, so that they will be empowered to make more of it happen than the megamachine would have planned — is one of the most important elements of 'what we want' in green education. It is a big field, and takes a while to get into, but here are a couple of tasters from Richard Slaughter, one of the most active curriculum developers of 'Futures'.

1 The future unfolds like a dice game

Every second, millions of things happen which could have happened another way and produced a different future. A scientist checks a spoiled culture and throws it away, or looks at it more closely and discovers penicillin. A spy at the Watergate removes a piece of tape from a door and gets away safely, or he forgets to remove the tape and changes American political history. Through such a random series of actions, the future chaotically emerges.

We must accept that chance plays a dominant role, accept the misfortune which comes our way and enjoy any good luck.

2 The future is like being on a roller coaster on a dark night

All of us are in a car on the roller coaster speeding along the rails. We know that we are on a fixed track which the car must follow, that our future is determined but we don't know where the track is going because everything is dark. Occasionally a flash of lightning exposes an approaching section of the track. We can see for an instant what will happen next. However, this does us very little good because we are locked in our seats and nothing we can do can change the course that is laid out for us.

3 The future is like a mighty river

We are in a boat on that river. There is a generally predetermined course — the river has definite banks and a strong current — but we have more freedom to steer than on a rollercoaster. We have to follow the river, but we can look ahead and avoid the whirlpools and sandbars. If the river forks, we can choose which direction we are to take; we must make a decision and then steer towards our destination.

4 The future is like a great ocean

We are on a ship in the ocean — there are many possible destinations and many different paths to each destination. We can choose whatever future we will, if we work for it; there are currents, storms and reefs to be dealt with but with care we can sail the ship to where we want to be.

Metaphors of time and the future

Time is a basic quality or condition of our lives. Our understanding of it is shaped by the language we use and there is a surprising number of common phrases involving time.

Time has been measured for many centuries but our notion of Western linear time is relatively recent. It only became dominant when clocks became widely available in the Middle Ages. Before this period time was much more closely associated with natural rhythms and cycles.

Our view of time suggests that it 'flows' in a one-way 'direction'. That is, from past to future. It is often embodied in the metaphor of a stream or river which bears us relentlessly forward and presents dangers which require careful navigation. Yet we are sometimes told not to 'waste' time — as if it were a quantity or resource. The saying 'time is money' reflects a particularly Western view and may contribute to the anxiety which is one of the features of Western linear time.

Other metaphors for time include the dice game and the rollercoaster. In the former case the assumption is that history is a result of sheer chance. In the second everything is predetermined and the important thing is to hang on and enjoy the ride.

Time is not a simple matter and no single metaphor or approach can describe it fully. As individuals we are always immersed in a particular web of metaphors about time. It is useful to become aware of how these shape our perception and to begin to consciously choose between a variety of interpretations. The following questions may help you to begin this process.

1. Illustrate three contrasting metaphors of time in three different pictures.

2. Choose some common sayings about time and comment upon their validity and usefulness.

3. Invent a metaphor which expresses your view of time. Describe some of the wider consequences of your metaphor becoming accepted.

4. What are the main benefits and drawbacks of Western linear time?

2: The political context

Green and red

Green teaching is a deeply political enterprise — that is the point of it. *The* creative political debate of the end of the twentieth century is that of the greens and the reds, and *Green Teacher* warmly welcomed that debate, as it refers to education, onto its pages. First, John Huckle, who teachers at Bedford College, asked 'Ten Red Questions to Ask Green Teachers', which lay down the groundwork for the discussion from the socialist point of view. Then Mike Thomas, of 'The Future in Our Hands' organisation, contributed a reply. Then David Pepper, geography lecturer at Oxford Polytechnic, offered the following educational perspectives.

The red–green debate is central to the important question of where we in education go from here. In the past 20 years consciousness about environmental issues, among decision-takers and the general public, has undoubtedly been raised. Many people in the educated West at least know that there are problems about the impacts which growth and consumerism have on the environment. They know about nuclear war and power, pollution, food quality, the countryside and the rest. Teachers have presented these as issues to the pupils, but the question is, do those pupils know what to do about them?

No. And neither does the green perspective in general offer any really viable course of action for them or for the mass of people, who are trapped by a specific economic system — capitalism — into the kinds of lifestyles which greens try to reject. Reds and greens generally agree on what is wrong (though the former believe that the latter's definition of 'environment' as vested largely in 'nature' is too narrow: for most of us the environment is essentially a social rather than a 'natural' thing). But on the crucial issue of how to bring about social change — including attitudinal changes — so many greens are deaf to arguments that take us beyond a very restricted world view: the world view of Western middle-classes.

Individualism

There is too much emphasis in the Western viewpoint on the efficacy of individual personal reform. People, through 'consciousness raising' and 'education', must miraculously become nicer — less competitive and more 'feminine', for example — in their attitudes to each other. And they must live out this 'niceness', perhaps in stark contrast to the selfishness of those around them. The proposition is that if only these selfish people knew what they were doing (to nature, etc) then they would stop doing it and start behaving very differently. Yet for most of us this is probably not true. And the idea that it is, furthermore, smacks of that very liberal philosophy that actually underpins the Western capitalist economy — a philosophy of bourgeois individualism, where society is seen merely as a collection of individuals with whom everything starts and finishes, and aggregate behaviour is explained in terms of the behaviour of the individual basic building blocks. As such it negates a very important part of human nature: that is our communal essence — a need to be part of, and intimately related to, other people. And hence it negates our potential for achieving social/attitudinal change through widespread collective action. Indeed, merely to live a virtuous, monk-like, non-material existence as an individual will not do much for the majority of people in the West, let alone the Third World. Far from showing them by example how to live, it frequently alienates them. However, collective action may draw them in to the way of changing their own lives.

Educational implications

The message for teachers is clear. We must enable and encourage pupils to find out about the political dimensions of environmental problems. We must show, for example, how Sahelian famine does not result from 'overpopulation' in a basically fertile land, but derives from the marginalisation of the Third World peasantry in favour of high-tech capital-intensive agriculture for the international market. This marginalisation, by which peasants are forced to deforest, overwork and erode the soil, has been politically produced, by capitalism.

Similarly, the capitalist organisation of industry produces externalities like pollution, but that does not mean that all industrialisation is bad as greens repeatedly suggest. It is perhaps possible to organise industrial production under a system — socialism — whereby social needs can be met, yet 'harmony' with nature can be sustained. Such questions must be addressed, as must the issues of individualism and competition versus commun(al)ism and co-operation. But having exposed the very political nature of the debate, teachers cannot stop there, if they are going to avoid inculcating the feeling of powerlessness that Thomas rightly wants to avoid. They must help pupils to see how, practically and collectively, they could achieve change of an ultimately revolutionary nature — in the short term through the extant political system of Parliamentary 'democracy', but also in the longer term through trades unionism, community group action and through organising and disseminating their own media, for example.

It probably is not largely a matter of 'teaching' the 'correct' values, as Thomas suggests. Education is about drawing out what is likely already to be there — not inculcation or indoctrination. If pupils are enabled to analyse the values behind their present socially-learned behaviour patterns they will conclude for themselves that different behaviour requires different values — and these will probably be values that they believe in at heart, because at heart most kids are decent and nice. What pupils need above all is to know how behaviour patterns can change, and such knowledge cannot be complete without some understanding of the relations of production that stem from our economics — relationships that substantially contribute to our behaviour patterns in the first place.

None of this is to say that the red–green debate is a matter simply of what produces (or determines) what: do economics produce values (red) or do values produce economics (green). It is not a question of which comes first, but is a chicken-and-egg problem. The relationship between ideas and material conditions in society is a dialectical one.

Each acts on the other constantly to change each side of the equation continuously. In fact there are not two separate 'sides' — ideas, values and attitudes are intimately linked to economic organisations and vice versa. So education, in changing individual and collective values, is important, too. It is a matter of balance, because such education cannot be isolated from the development of political and economic consciousness. And education must go beyond consciousness, to the practical. Part of the practical involves a knowledge of how to use the prevailing political system to advantage — how to campaign to (a) shift views and policies within a party, (b) get that party into power. Merely to limit practical action to the kind of examples which Thomas suggests — 'fund-raising for Third World charities' or 'paper collection for recycling' is to sustain the present power elite and the conventional wisdom on which that elite's power is based. So to avoid 'political party bickering' in schools, as Thomas puts it, is to practice a deception. For there is a big difference between the parties even today, let alone in their historical roots. Labour does have a far better environmental programme and outlook than do the Conservatives; the Alliance is a hopeless mish-mash of cluttered thinking, and the Green party will not get power in Britain in the forseeable future. These are the immediate realities that must be addressed.

But practical political education goes much further than this, and may involve teaching pupils how to live, work and produce co-operatively, and how to start by doing so rather than entering the rat race when they leave school. And they should be shown how to support and develop local government to the extent that a truly decentralist 'municipal socialism', as Huckle describes, can be established (this is not a pipe-dream vision of the same order as the anarchist utopias of which greens are so fond: and we have begun already to approach it through the work of the so-called 'looney left' councils).

Conventional versus 'alternative' education

Can practical political education be achieved through the conventional education system, or will there have to be 'alternative' schools and colleges? Is, by definition, the first system destined for failure if, as in Huckle's materialist analysis, education today is largely a way of perpetrating the ideas and values that support the dominant class in society? The answer is, most certainly, that this is not so.

If the relationship between values and economic conditions is dialectical, so too is the relationship between social institutions (like education) and economic conditions. This means that there is scope to change the institutions by reform and argument, and in their changed state they can have an effect on the material organisation of society. But the extent of change in the former will be limited without change in the latter, so, practically, educational

reform will be difficult, given syllabus constraints imposed
increasingly from the political centre, and given the conditions in
which teachers work: struggling merely to maintain some form of
discipline and to meet the commitment to a high level of contact
hours. But 'difficult' does not mean 'impossible'. As Huckle points
out, the new GCSE and proposed A-level syllabuses leave room for
more than one interpretation of what constitutes social
responsibility and relevance. And they also positively encourage
the growth of active rather than passive pupil involvement in
teaching methods — a condition just ripe for the development of

critical and questioning approaches to the premises underlying conventional capitalist wisdom.

Furthermore, teachers do not have to start from scratch when it comes to deciding what to teach, and how to teach it, within the broad frameworks laid down by school curricula. There are many examples of teaching approaches and classroom exercises that are geared to the kind of educational issues and perspectives that greens want to explore. The Association for Curriculum Development or the Geography 16–19 project constitute but two examples of the many teacher organisations that produce such materials.

Additionally, teachers who agree on the need to raise political consciousness among pupils should also be politically active themselves — not just in local environmental politics, but in the processes and the machinery that lead to the production of curricula in the first place. It is right and proper to strike about teachers' pay; but it is equally right and proper to strike against current government moves to centralise and dictate curricula.

There is, then, much scope within the conventional system, and any incremental gains that are made are likely to be far-reaching, given the fact that most children are educated within that system.

However, there is also scope for the development of 'alternative' educational patterns (de-schooling in favour of education in living communities, for example) and institutions (like 'green'/socialist schools and colleges) where, at least in theory, many of the constraints on teachers inside the system do not exist. There may be many reservations about them — for example they require much work, clear thinking and organisational flair to establish and run, especially if they do not immediately gain the respect and support of trained and experienced people within the system, and at the end of that work they may be mainly preaching to small numbers of the already-converted. Furthermore, if they develop curricula and course that display the over-idealism and over-individualist philosophy that characterises so much mainstream green thinking, then they may be making a rather limited contribution to fundamental social change, for reasons given above. In their favour, however, they do represent opportunities for radically new departures, and many of the respected and established institutions of today, such as the Steiner Schools, Dartington Hall, or even Birkbeck and Ruskin colleges, are the 'alternative' educational institutions of yesterday.

Again, however, it is towards the Socialist and Labour movement that such would-be alternative institutions might turn in their struggle to effect social change. For, despite the popular image of this movement, it has been in the forefront of educational reform in the past, demanding and assisting with resources for such reform. For their part, socialists in the Labour movement (and there are many) should revive this tradition of insisting on, and paying for, truly progressive education: both within and outside the system. There must be a dialectic between red and green movements in Britain. In the past it has been the socialists who have been reluctant to join that dialectic. Now, I fear, the reluctance comes from the other side, and not, certainly, from the rank-and-file of the Labour movement. Greens must overcome their reluctance, and clear thinking about the dynamics of our current — capitalist — society might constitute the first step.

[David Pepper, *Green Teacher* 4]

Ten key values

This set of questions, mentioned in the paragraphs about Charlene Spretnak in Chapter 4, has been used widely in the last three years, particularly in the USA, as the focus for green political discussion. I have used them very successfully as a resource for seminar work with 17-year-olds.

1. Ecological wisdom

How can we operate human societies with the understanding that we are part of nature, not on top of it? How can we live within the ecological and resource limits of the planet, applying our technological knowledge to the challenge of an energy-efficient economy? How can we build a better relationship between cities and countryside? How can we guarantee the rights of nonhuman species? How can we promote sustainable agriculture and respect for self-regulating natural systems? How can we further biocentric wisdom in all spheres of life?

2. Grassroots democracy

How can we develop systems that allow and encourage us to control the decisions that affect our lives? How can we ensure that representatives will be fully accountable to the people who elect them? How can we develop planning mechanisms that would allow citizens to develop and implement their own preferences for policies and spending priorities? How can we encourage and assist the 'mediating institutions' — family, neighbourhood organisation, church group, voluntary association, ethnic club — to recover some of the functions now performed by government? How can we relearn the best insights from American traditions of civic vitality, voluntary action, and community responsibility?

3. Personal and social responsibility?

How can we respond to human suffering in ways that promote dignity? How can we encourage people to commit themselves to lifestyles that promote their own health? How can we have a community-controlled education system that effectively teaches our children academic skills, ecological wisdom, social responsibility, and personal growth? How can we resolve interpersonal and intergroup conflicts without just turning them over to lawyers and judges? How can we take responsibility for reducing the crime rate in our neighbourhoods? How can we encourage such values as simplicity and moderation?

4. Non-violence

How can we, as a society, develop effective alternatives to our current patterns of violence, at all levels, from the family and the street to nations and the world? How can we eliminate nuclear weapons from the face of the Earth without being naïve about the intentions of other governments? How can we most constructively use non-violent methods to oppose practices and policies with which we disagree, and in the process reduce the atmosphere of polarization and selfishness that is itself a source of violence?

5. Decentralisation

How can we restore power and responsibility to individuals, institutions, communities, and regions? How can we encourage the flourishing of regionally-based culture rather than a dominant monoculture? How can we have a decentralised, democratic society with our political, economic, and social institutions, locating power on the smallest scale (closest to home) that is efficient and practical? How can we redesign our institutions so that fewer

decisions and less regulation over money are granted as one moves
from the community toward the national level? How can we
reconcile the need for community and regional self-determination
with the need for appropriate centralised regulation in certain
matters?

6. Community-based economics

How can we redesign our work structures to encourage employee
ownership and workplace democracy? How can we develop new
economic activities and institutions that will allow us to use our
new technologies in ways that are humane, freeing, ecological,
and accountable, and responsive to communities? How can we
establish some form of basic economic security, open to all? How
can we move beyond the narrow 'job ethic' to new definitions of
'work', 'jobs' and 'income' that reflect the changing economy? How
can we restructure our patterns of income distribution to reflect the
wealth created by those outside the formal, monetary economy:
those who take responsibility for parenting, housekeeping, home
gardens, community volunteers work, etc? How can we restrict the
size and concentrated power of corporations without discouraging
superior efficiency or technological innovation?

7. Post-patriarchal values

How can we replace the cultural ethics of dominance and control
with more co-operative ways of interacting? How can we
encourage people to care about persons outside their own group?
How can we promote the building of respectful, positive, and
responsible relationships across the lines of gender and other
divisions? How can we encourage a rich, diverse political culture
that respects feelings as well as rationalist approaches? How can
we proceed with as much respect for the means as the end (the
process as much as the products of our efforts)? How can we learn
to respect the contemplative, inner part of life as much as the outer
activities?

8. Respect for diversity

How can we honor cultural, ethnic, racial, sexual, religious and
spiritual diversity within the context of individual responsibility
toward all beings? How can we reclaim our country's finest shared

ideals: the dignity of the individual, democratic participation, and liberty and justice for all?

9. Global responsibility

How can we be of genuine assistance to grassroots groups in the Third World? What can we learn from such groups? How can we help other countries make the transition to self-sufficiency in food and other basic necessities? How can we cut our defence budget while maintaining an adequate defence? How can we promote these ten green values in the reshaping of global order? How can we reshape world order without creating just another enormous nation-state?

10. Future focus

How can we induce people and institutions to think in terms of the long-range future, and not just in terms of their short-range selfish interest? How can we encourage people to develop their own visions of the future and move more effectively toward them? How can we judge whether new technologies are socially useful — and use those judgements to shape our society? How can we induce our government and other institutions to practice fiscal responsibility? How can we make the quality of life, rather than open-ended economic growth, the focus of future thinking?

[*Green Teacher* 7]

Leaked manifesto?

This document came to light in the pages of a *New Internationalist* issue on education. It was written by Robin Richardson, who was an advisor on multi-cultural education in Berkshire and is now principal advisor in the London borough of Brent. Rings true, doesn't it?

Preamble

1. We hold this truth to be self-evident: that human beings are created unequal.
2. There is amongst us inequality of talent, intelligence and virtue; of capacity to enjoy freedom and create wealth; and of the

ability to rule, lead, organise and contribute to an ordered, harmonious and decent society.

3. Grave threats are posed to our civilisation by those who preach the pernicious gospel that inequality is neither right nor inevitable. They include not only atheistic and communistic states on the international scene but also certain people within our own scoiety. Their ideas gain plausibility amongst the idle, the envious and the unlettered. They must be vigorously suppressed.

4. The country's education system has a vital role to play in hallowing, protecting and furthering inequality. We therefore propose the nine-point plan that follows. Its goal is to return the British education system to its historic and essential task, which is that of preparing the young to take up their rightful places in society as either leaders or led, and to accept, appreciate, and enjoy their inequality.

A nine-point plan for educational reform

1. National curriculum

We will ensure that all schools teach the same basic subjects. We propose 10 such subjects, to act as foundation stones for the society which we wish to build and maintain. The subjects will, of course, be kept entirely separate from, and therefore uncontaminated by, each other.

2. Testing

We will ensure that all children have their memories for each of the foundation subjects tested at the ages of 7, 11, 13 and 16. The results of these tests will be published, so that inequalities of talent and memorising ability are entirely plain. This will also ensure that, from the earliest stages, children are groomed for competition.

3. Local control

We will ensure that each school is controlled by a Board of Governors. This Board will supervise the local introduction of the national curriculum, and the local publication of test results. Its members will be drawn from groups sympathetic to the ideals and principles of inequality: in particular from the senior management of large-scale industry and commerce but also, of course, from local police forces.

A note on terminology

We recognise that the term 'local controllers' may not have the friendly image which we wish to project. Accordingly we propose that the local controllers and supervisors of schools should normally be referred to as 'parents'.

4. Controversy

We will ensure that, so far as possible, teachers avoid teaching about controversial subjects. Most of the time the new national curriculum will itself prevent controversy arising. But certain teachers may lack the competence and expertise to avoid controversy completely. Such teachers will be expected to follow carefully the following guidelines:

(i) **Sex:** The proper place for women is the home, and the education of girls must always bear this in mind. Sexual activity, other than within marriage, is usually immoral, frequently deviant and invariably regrettable.

(ii) **Religion:** Christianity is clearly superior to all other religions, or so-called religions.

(iii) **Politics:** There is no place in schools for extremist political views, for example views which question the principles in this manifesto.

5. Culture

We will ensure that British values are paramount. The curriculum and ethos of our schools, the textbooks that are used, the displays, everything, must reflect and sustain pride in our nation and all things British. Immigrants must be made very clear about this. The term 'education for racial equality', incidentally, is highly inflammatory and implies an aggressive campaign designed to brainwash people: it must not be used.

6. Removal of opposition

Our only remotely significant opponents are certain locally-elected politicians, aided and abetted by various unrepresentative members of the teaching force, and by a number of misguided education officers and politicised advisers. We will ensure that their influence is severely curtailed and, if possible, removed. We therefore intend a package of measures to achieve this, including delegation of financial decisions and appointment of teaching staff to local controllers (known as 'parents' — see item 3 above), and central Government support for individual schools which have been particularly successful at promoting inequality. This latter measure will be known as 'opting out'.

7. Ladders to success

We will ensure that a number of carefully selected children from poor homes, including perhaps even some children or grandchildren of immigrants, are allowed to succeed at school, and to go to university. This will demonstrate to everyone that our educational system is fair and just, and will help generate gratitude, loyalty and affection.

8. The arts

We will ensure that access to literature, religion and the creative arts is limited to those few children who are capable of appreciating them, and whose parents can afford to pay the extra costs involved. We will guard vigorously against the danger of allowing immature minds to 'express' themselves or to be 'imaginative', 'playful', 'prophetic' or 'satirical'.

9. Complementary measures

We will ensure that our educational reforms are strengthened by other legislation which we are introducing to increase inequality — in particular, our measures to reduce public expenditure on health, housing and welfare benefits, and to curb the powers of trade unions. Insofar as our education reforms are not immediately successful we shall be happy, indeed keen, to introduce the following:
(i) Compulsory military service, to complete the education of those who fail at school.
(ii) Reduced taxes on alcohol, tranquilizers and burglar alarms.
(iii) Humane psychiatric treatment for members of the teaching force who are unable to cope.
(iv) A much enlarged police force.

Consultation

This draft manifesto has been issued for public consultation. However, the closing date for the receipt of your comments has unfortunately passed.

[*New Internationalist* 180, February 1988, p. 21]

How's your crap detector?

Bob Stradling researches and writes on the teaching of controversial issues. There follows an extract from his article on 'Teaching Green Issues'.

It is not surprising that decision-makers at all levels, operating with these considerable advantages, and unduly protected by an atmosphere of obsessive secrecy (commercial as well as governmental) are able to disseminate misinformation and disinformation, procrastinate on vital issues, and prevent issues of public concern from receiving a fair and open hearing. If readers feel that I am overstating my case I suggest that they take a close look at the press releases of the Central Electricity Generating Board and British Nuclear Fuels Ltd over the past few years, regarding the operations of nuclear power reactors and re-processing plants.

In these circumstances one would question whether policy-makers are in a position to make rational judgements based on the information available to them, let alone the ordinary public. Ultimately these 'rational judgements' rest upon non-rational trust in the veracity of our sources. If this analysis of the current situation is accurate then it could have certain major implications for the teaching of those green issues that are highly controversial, contemporary and, as yet, unresolved.

First, I would suggest that we need to help young people develop their own 'built-in crap detectors'. This means learning how to ask good, searching questions and how to detect poor, misleading or evasive answers. Teasing out people's taken-for-granted assumptions; considering what we would need to know in order to substantiate such assumptions; critically examining the public utterances of those who wish to persuade us to their point of view for evidence to back up their claims; and distinguishing between information that can be substantiated by sources not connected to the original source, and information that we are expected to take on trust — all these represent the investigative style of thinking encapsulated by the phrase 'crap detection'.

This indicates a process-based rather than a product-based approach to the teaching of issues. The emphasis is less on the acquisition of knowledge and more on the learning of 'take-away skills', which the students will be able to apply to any future controversial issue they might encounter.

Second, we need to encourage students to apply a 'green perspective' to relevant issues. As long as this perspective is marginalised by those within the mass media who have editorial control and by those in official quarters who have the power to set the agenda for political debate, then a state of unfair competition exists between alternative ideas and points of view. It is not too difficult to identify a dominant perspective on environmental issues and problems. It may be characterised as promoting an unshakeable faith in the technological fix, i.e. that the problems confronting humanity are all capable of being solved by technological and scientific advances. It portrays those who question the alleged benefits of technology as Luddites and cranks. It propagates the belief that the only appropriate measure of the efficient use of natural and human resources is 'value for money'. It presents civilisation as the progressive taming of nature. And it advances the economists' narrow view of human nature in which people are assumed to be interested only in maximising their own short-term personal gains and minimising their losses.

By contrast, I would suggest that the central organising concept of a green perspective is the quality of life. I am not advocating here that this perspective should be promoted in a proselytising way by teachers — that seems to me to be miseducative and probably counter-productive, since most students seem to switch off mentally when their teachers start peddling their principles. Instead they ought to be encouraged to broaden the criteria which they or the mass media or policy-makers apply when thinking about what ought to be done. For example, when the Department of Energy claims that one particular source of fuel is cheaper than the other, have they included in their calculations the ecological costs, the social costs and the research and development costs? The LEA and DES guidelines on teaching issues assert that the teacher's objective should be to encourage rational judgement on such issues.

[*Green Teacher* 3]

3: Learning by growing

Lifelab

This is an amazing project based in Santa Cruz, California, which helps teachers and children to base their science (or most of their curriculum, including Maths and English and Arts, depending on how ambitiously they use it) on 'learning by growing'.

The ultimate goal, to quote Lifelab leader Gary Appel, is to 'provoke curiosity about the world and the fragile complexity of its natural order, to satisfy that curiosity through observation and learning, and to create an understanding of our place in the ecological structure and our responsibility to it.'

I visited Lifelab in 1986 and have been telling everyone about it ever since. The three books of curriculum (Americanism) are one of the most precious resources a green teacher could possess.

[*Green Teacher* 2]

What good is compost? . . . or, what hath rot wrought?

Purpose

To determine the effects of compost on plant growth.

Materials

Garden bed or planter box, seeds or seedlings.

Action

1. Plants have to eat too! They need a good balanced diet, just like people. Compost provides a healthy combination of important nutrients, like nitrogen, potassium, and phosphorus. Let's see if compost helps plants grow.

2. Divide the bed (or box) in half and mark it off with string. Fertilize one half with ample amounts of compost, and the other half

not at all. Plant the whole bed with one crop. Another possibility is to dig two beds, preparing only one with compost, and planting several kinds of the same types of crops in each bed:

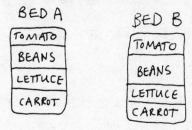

BED A
| TOMATO |
| BEANS |
| LETTUCE |
| CARROT |

BED B
| TOMATO |
| BEANS |
| LETTUCE |
| CARROT |

It doesn't matter which crops you choose, but try to pick at least one root crop, one leaf crop, and one fruit crop.

3. Make charts comparing the success of each crop in the two beds. You could compare their germination, speed of growth, health as they grow, and their final size and taste when they are harvested!

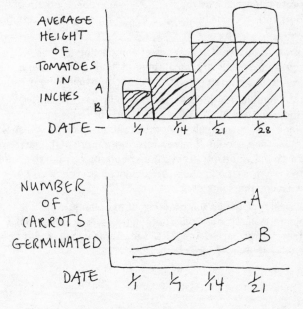

4. Summarise your information at the end of the experiment. Which bed did better? If it was the one with the compost, why did it do better? Do people also grow better with better nutrition? Do they grow bigger, faster, and have fewer 'pest' problems?

To dig or not to dig; that is the question

Purpose
To discover the effect of compaction on plant growth.

Materials
Seeds or seedlings, a garden bed that has been double-dug but not fertilised, and a compacted area (like a path) nearby.

Action

1. The following can be read to students as background: We double-dig in order to make the soil less compacted. Compacted means dense, or packed closely together. When soil is compacted, there is less room for air, water doesn't drain out (so roots rot), and seedlings have a hard time pushing through the soil.

2. Discuss with students the causes of compaction (people walking, cows grazing, machinery, etc.). Remind them that we avoid walking on our garden beds to prevent compacting them.

3. Plant the double-dug (Bed A) and the compacted area (Bed B) with the same amounts of the same kinds of seeds (or seedlings). Try to keep all other factors the same: the soil should be similar (one shouldn't have much more nutrients); watering should be the same, etc. They should both be planted the same, thinned if necessary. In short, both planted areas should be given exactly the same care.

4. Make weekly notes on the progress of the plants: which germinate faster, grow faster, get bigger, look healthier, have less insect or disease damage? Did more plants survive in one place than another? Make charts:

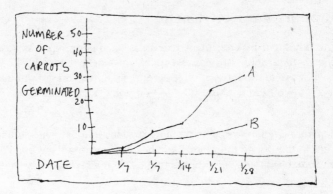

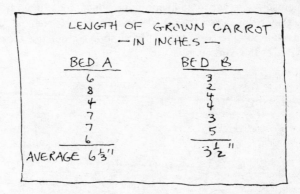

5. When the crops mature, review your charts on each vegetable. Which bed did better? Most likely the double-dug bed will produce the healthiest plants. Review the reasons why it is important to loosen the soil.

6. Ask students to stick out their finger and pretend it has become a seed. Have them try to push their seed-finger into a compacted area. They should really push around and feel how hard it is. Now ask them to sink their seed-finger into a double-dug bed. Finally ask them to 'plant' their finger-seed where they think it would grow the best.

Support your city farm!

The city farm movement of Britain is an unsung success story.
Enormous amounts of earnest idealism have produced a string
of what are extremely valuable resources. Have you got one near
you? Do you know about it? Are you going to find out?

There are city farms and community gardens in most major urban
areas in the United Kingdom. Land has been restored and buildings
renovated — the city has started to grow in the real sense of the
word.

They are projects that are set up and managed by local people
for themselves, creating an invigorating effect on community self-
help. They have shown themselves to be a popular channel for
those attempting to come together to improve amenities for
everyone in the community.

One of the unwritten rules of city farming is that there should be
five good reasons for doing something. However, there are many
more than this for setting up a city farm or community garden:

- By visiting their city farm regularly, children see plants and
  animals as a natural part of their lives: indeed, in these times
  of intensive farming and agribusiness, children on a city farm
  are often closer to animals than many of their country cousins.

- For all children the contact with plants and animals and people
  in a relaxed, supportive but work-like environment is an
  important stimulus to their personal development.

- We take many placements from a variety of hostels, hospitals, support projects and other agencies, and visits from sheltered workshops, special schools and other welfare institutions.

- City farms and community gardens may also offer work experience, and may sponsor Youth Training and employment projects through the Manpower Services Commission programmes.

- We provide a new focus for the elderly in an area, a place where they are welcomed as valued members of the community, and can share their life experiences.

- We reintroduce an ecological balance to urban areas. We are an important vehicle, along with work by specialist conservation groups, for protecting the latent ecology of urban areas.

- We ensure that most, if not all, gardening facilities are accessible to all people irrespective of their disadvantage or disability. The deaf, the visually impaired and the mentally handicapped derive great enjoyment from their visits, and their needs are also taken into account in the livestock and gardening areas of city farms.

- City farms are real working farms in an animal husbandry sense rather than an economic one — they may not be self-supporting in terms of produce but they do aim to be as self-financing as is possible through the services they offer.

- Open space on projects allows carnivals, dances, celebrations and other community events to take place.

- City farms are cost-effective, because they involve volunteers, receive donations both in cash and in kind, and raise and manage money by their own efforts.

- All projects have the potential of generating permanent jobs that provide a real service to the local community.

- By adopting the principles of sustainable agriculture, they improve the environment, reduce costs, and achieve productive cropping on previously derelict sites.

- City farms are there to meet local needs, all of which are not necessarily apparent in the early stages. Some begin by emphasising children, others the elderly, but each project evolves into a true focus for the local community.

In fact, there are as many reasons for having a city farm or community garden as there are people in the local community.

[*Green Teacher* 2]

Ecological parks

Science in the primary curriculum has brought about a lot of long-needed inservice training and development of resources. But if teachers and parents work together, the urban ecological park, born in 1977 with an idea of Max Nicholson, could become a major resource in every town and city.

Pam Morris, who writes here, ran the educational work at the William Curtis Ecological Park in East London from 1981 to 1985.

This article is addressed to people living and working in the inner cities and to all concerned with the quality of life in the 20th century.

Fortunately, within the city, people exist such as Max Nicholson, Chairman of the Trust for Urban Ecology, who in 1977 had the visionary idea of creating Britain's first ecological park in the heart of London.

The William Curtis Ecological Park was set up by theTrust with the express intention of promoting a greater understanding of urban ecology. One obvious target was to involve local schools in the management and study of the Park. This became my task from May 1981 until the Park's closure, due to site redevelopment, in July 1985. At the end of this period I came away with the conviction that the Park had fulfilled its role, and that similar but permanent centres should be set up throughout the country in the near future.

Why?

When I took up my appointment we had only the bare bones of an educational centre (Adam's rib?).

Conditions:

- a two-acre park containing a patchwork of habitats — woodlands, sand-dune, meadows, grassland, scrub, pond (see Figure 3).
- a hut with recycled tables, a few chairs, shelving, workbench and of course the kettle, plus a *Plurococcus*-infected water container.
- a classroom — the field.
- toilets — the bushes in summer, winter the basement.
- indoor shelter — an enormous sheet of polythene, found in a

nearby street, draped over the main entrance gate in inclement weather.

Resources

- two wardens — one a plant ecologist, one an animal ecologist — their knowledge, their reference material, their equipment.
- myself: a primary-trained teacher with ten years' experience working in inner city schools.

Survival strategy:

- beg, borrow, make, scrounge. . . .

Behaviour:

- doing what comes naturally — pond dipping, bird watching, mini-beast hunting, fungus foraying, bonfire building, ice-skating, tree planting, weeding . . . all with primary children and their teachers.

Of course, things improved. The Greater London Council donated a Portakabin classroom and Portaloo. The Inner London Education Authority gave furniture, a small annual allowance and the loan of books from teachers' centres. Benefactors stepped in. Posters, postcards, and badges of the Park were produced and sold at a small profit. Schools made donations, while many teachers suffered temporary amnesia when it came to rounding up paper, pencils, paints, plasticine and later tape measures, balances, thermometers — the list and their support are both endless.

Why was it that under such primitive conditions (which we all took for granted), teachers used the Park with ever-increasing regularity between the years 1981 and 1985? From replies to a questionnaire sent to these teachers, we were able to identify their main reason: the presence of site-based staff who were willing to help them plan and work with their pupils during their visits. Because the wardens and myself kept day-to-day diaries of the educational and ecological use of the Park, we had access to a data base from which we could predict patterns of change in the flora and fauna, and plan educational use accordingly.

When a school was due to visit we would either ring to see if we could match work being carried out in the classroom, or the school would ring us to ask what they could expect to find at that time of

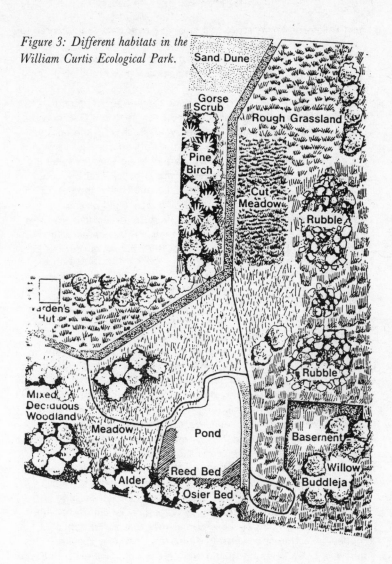

Figure 3: Different habitats in the William Curtis Ecological Park.

the year. Many teachers, after a long day at school, would come to see for themselves what was around. This was followed by small talk over cups of coffee then back to business, to clarify aims and to work out what preparation was necessary at school and at the Park.

This system of preparatory visits took a number of years to achieve, mainly because publicity had been sent to all ILEA schools prior to my appointment. In my first year, figures for the number of educational establishments using the Park soared, but I was not happy with the situation. I felt we were chasing quantity (vital if we were to justify future funding) rather than quality. I felt we could maintain our figures, but could do so by publicising the Park to local schools. In doing so we could give local children the opportunity to come into contact with nature throughout the term, throughout the year and throughout their primary careers, thus gaining maximum benefit not only for the children but for the Park itself.

Consolidation

By 1985 we were well on the way towards achieving these aims. What's more, local children began using the Park in their leisure hours. Some came to continue work carried out in lesson time, others to chat with site staff, while the majority came simply to play — especially once we had locked up for the evening. We rarely saw these children, but they did leave evidence of their visits: discarded and forgotten clothing lying around the pond margin, BMX tracks through the meadows, camps and bows and arrows in the bushes — reminders of our own childhood experiences with nature.

In addition, parents began to use the Park as a sanctuary and safe play area for their toddlers on hot summer's days. Office workers came in their lunch breaks and could often be seen 'helping' the children, especially when their work centred around the pond. And of course there was always the 'boffin bonus', a motley collection of scientists visiting the Park for a specific purpose, often using intriguing equipment which we asked them to explain to the fascinated pupils.

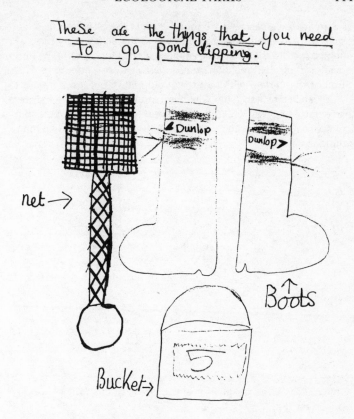

These are the things that you need to go pond dipping.

net →

Dunlop

Dunlop →

Boots ↑

Bucket →

In praise of the Curtis frog (or teaching frog ecology)

What then of teaching ecology? In order to do so we needed to structure our work. What we chose to use were the aims and objectives outlined in Macdonalds' *Science 5/14* publications — the ones produced on behalf of the Schools' Council, which are a great confidence booster for anyone starting out on primary science for the first time.

Towards the end of the spring term children could see literally hundreds of frogs, mainly adults males and females, making their way to the pond. The differences between them were obvious once detected and discussed. Their courtship behaviour evoked discussion which could be summarised as survival of the fittest. The moral question on whether they could be handled arose. In certain years carcasses were found around the pond margin, especially after particularly cold spells. Children were asked to suggest factors that might be responsible for their mortality and to question their own reaction, which was always to bury them. Should we interfere with nature? Could nature put these deaths to some use? Once courtship was over, large areas of the pond were blanketed in spawn. Children attempted to estimate the potential number of offspring, and wondered why frogs produced so many young.

We had two main reasons for encouraging pupils to take spawn back to school:

1. Spawning tended to coincide with the Easter holidays. If it wasn't removed the pond would receive a hammering from less-aware children intent only on collecting it.
2. Here was an opportunity for pupils to observe and record changes over a relatively short period of time — changes that would be spectacular enough to sustain their interest.

Work began in the Park, continued at school and was taken up again at Curtis when they returned their froglets. Of course most of the children wanted to put the froglets into the pond — hardly surprising — fairy stories have frogs in ponds. Even nature books show them sitting on lily pads, and we were occasionally treated to this enchanting spectacle.

We used the opportunity to dispel a 'wildlife myth'. Armed with clipboard, maps of the Park and tally charts the children set off in small groups to investigate the presence or absence of frogs in all habitats, including of course the pond. Limited by time each group was given two habitats to investigate. Their findings were reported to other groups. Why were they where they had been found? Perhaps their food was there. Time for more ideas from the children and research into reference books to see what froglets ate, then back into the field to see if there was a match between 'frog place' and 'frog food'. And so into the Autumn term when frog sightings became rare and children suggested they were probably hibernating. However, they knew, as a result of their own experiences that next Spring the wheel would have turned and they could renew their favourite activity of 'frog watching'.

There is growing pressure on primary teachers to teach science. To help them respond effectively, help must be provided in the form of teacher training and the provision of resources. When Curtis closed we lost a centre that gave inspiration to others, offered inner city children a safe place in which to play, was used for relaxation by workers and members of the community, and provided a sanctuary for London's wildlife. Not only this but it was prized as a valuable educational resource by local primary teachers.

In creating the William Curtis Ecological Park, the Trust for Urban Ecology blazed a trail for others to follow. The question to be answered is, Will they?

[*Green Teacher* 3]

4: The inner person

Dancing into the wild

Gordon MacLellan is a countryside warden at an outdoor education centre in Manchester. He is clearly interested in extending the usual definitions of his work. . . .

Somewhere inside everyone there is a dancer. Tucked away, often deeply hidden, in the depths of the lumbering or double-footed teacher and the quietest fumble-shy pupil there is a dancer, bouncing away into eternity.

Our dancers, cupboard-locked inside our heads are all individual: all reflections of the individual self. Just as every person experiences the world in their own unique way, so every dancer moves to their own tune and every step in the dances of all these lives is unique. In our relationships with the environment, releasing the 'dancer within' can be a potent and rewarding way of developing that relationship. Dancing into the wild can touch the inner self through the creative, physical, freedom it represents. Personal ecology: as the self awakes and realises its own intrinsic value, so it, hopefully, comes to realise the value of the world to which it belongs.

With the advent of 'Earth Education' and similar approaches from other stables, environmental education is broadening its scope. Recognition is at last growing of the value of 'awareness'. The individual's personal relationship with the environment is at least the equal of the older 'record, examine and analyse' approach. The right of any individual to explore that personal relationship is being cultivated and this is not some philosophical pursuit for 'adults' but a valid aspect of every child's development.

In this atmosphere of exploration and adventure, dance works like the ripple of hands on a drum. In this article I would like to suggest ways of reaching out and entering the environment through dance, and with that, perhaps, touching the dancer within.

Ideas

Don't call it 'dance', for a start! That can invite too many prejudices about who dances, and how, and why. Perhaps do not even formally introduce it at all — get things started and let the ideas flow.

Everyone can dance, but maybe no-one ever offered this child or that what they needed to let themselves dance. Start by looking for everyone's own rhythm, their own heartbeats to the world. Try using sticks, bags of leaves, a box of gravel — anything you can find, and let everyone make a noise. Out of this bedlam, as leader, try to lift a group rhythm (a cardboard box drum, or scavenged plastic tub might be helpful here) and go for a procession: a hopping, skipping, dancing chain through your site.

This group cacophony could hive off into individual, or small group work. Go for the music, and the movement of, say, leaves falling, a beetle running, a shrew eating, and there is a dance already.

Freeform dance like this could develop into wider projects, drawing in expressive work in more media. At the risk of being anthropomorphic, try characterising the environment (or perhaps

this might be a good way of breaking some of that
anthropocentrism).

Make masks, or even whole costumes, out of what you can find —
fallen leaves, garden plants, dry grasses, dry rubbish (paper cups
and crisp packets can be amazing!). Animate your site. Let people
sit alone to think about their characters: Who are they? What is
their role in the local environment? How do they interact with all
their fellows? Then use a drum, or a recorder, or a rattle, to give
your group a rhythm and bring them dancing as their characters
out of their corners. Gather into a circle and take it from there.

Circle, or Sacred, Dance groups are established in many parts of
the country now and the Circle Dance repertoire of traditional
dances from a wide range of cultures offers the environmental
dance group a wonderful flowerbed to gather blossoms from.

The expression of natural cycles and relationships can be found
in elemental dances like the Irish 'King of the Fairies' (What does
a plant need for growth? Earth, water, air and sunlight, or fire).

The patterns that people have made out of the natural world can
turn out all sorts of things: footwork mandalas, questions: Why?
How? Can we make our own dances? In some dances a natural link

is clear in the movement, as in 'Snakes' from Serbia and 'Bears' from Latvia. In others, like the Greek 'Tsakonikos', the crane courtship of the original inspiration seems lost until you see a whole chain of dancers following its strange lilting movement: carefully shifting like the rise and fall of fanned wings.

There are all the dances that can fit in anywhere: corn-planting dances, a midwinter spiral dance, 'Banish Misfortune' at Hallowe'en, or one to thank the earth for a cheerful afternoon. Finally, there are those hop, skip, jump and *let's do it again* dances that are a joy to do and a laughter to fall over in, simply because they are fun to do.

The possibilities in dance are immense, both in free movement and through established dances, where it's not so much a question of memorising all the correct bits as enjoying the dance and following its feel. Children generally seem to enjoy dancing, if only for the novelty of dancing in the middle of a field. Who knows if we can find the 'dancer-within'? I don't, I only hope. And for older folks there is the chance to dance a child back into your heart and get that laughter and excitement going again (if it had ever left).

'At the still centre of things, there the dance is.'

Go for it.

[Green Teacher 8]

Musical rainforests

Ecological concerns visit the music room more rarely, it is a fair bet, then the science area or the humanities block. Sarah Maidlow contributed this inspiring example of 'eco-musicology'.

My stimulus was a booklet presented in one of the Sunday papers a couple of years ago, followed by two quite different films that both included people native to the forests living in harmony with the environment. The plight of the rainforest areas was clearly brought home. The devastating effects and pointlessness of their ruthless destruction for all sorts of short-term and inappropriate projects was upsetting — but in music lessons?

The answer was staring me in the face when I realised what it meant when the forest is considered in layers. It had clarified things for me, why not for the kids? And in musical terms it seemed ideal.

[I came across rainforest destruction at the point when our second years (12+) had just begun some lessons encouraging them to experiment with sound for its own sake. Using the topic in an adult workshop of about 2 hours it has worked fine without the preparatory work.]

Introduction

Our approach is to play a game, in which teams direct a blindfolded member to catch, or avoid being caught, by giving directions in abstract sound only (i.e. no words). For the first lesson, only 'body' sounds are available (although furniture sometimes comes into it). The game tends to push the children towards originality, otherwise their 'cat/mouse' gets confused by signals from the other team.

In the next lesson instruments can be used, although I tend to recommend that at least some people continue to use their voices. Having obtained some interesting and contrasted sounds, work then progresses to the 'opposite', where one person uses signals to direct the same sounds, in other words having a conductor. The children discover how difficult it can be, not having any idea what comes next, or trying to remember the sequence if they go for a 'worked out' piece. (Unless work is being taped we generally perform to each other, when appropriate, at the end of lessons, whatever the topic).

So now comes a nice quiet lesson. We have large rolls of wonderful free, (and tree-saving?) paper from a local printer, and the 'teams' work on table-lengths of it to produce pictorial scores of their piece from the previous lesson. I introduce this stage with a little lecture on the need to be aware of five elements of contrast:

- **rhythm**/duration of notes — long and short;
- **melody**/pitch — high and low;
- **dynamic**/volume — loud and quiet;
- **speed**/beat — fast and slow;
- **timbre**/sound quality (always the hardest to explain, yet often the first decision, i.e. 'What instrument shall I choose?')

They try to work out ways of indicating all this information on the score. Depending on the length of the project, an interesting lesson is asking groups to go round playing from each other's scores.

The rainforests

I start with an attempt at a general description of the environment, including a few of the amazing statistics like size and the numbers of species, trying to build a feeling for its all-embracing nature. (This is a good spot for a bit of video-showing and associated work with geographers and biologists, if you've got access). I don't say anything about destruction at this point, wanting people to become absorbed in the topic first. I show them a diagram of the layers, with some idea of the relative heights:

> emergents
> canopy
> sub-canopy
> shrubs
> seedlings

We then talk about the kinds of creatures that live at the different levels.

Working in groups, they next make (and note down) decisions on the overall piece. Each layer has to have a general plan, appropriate to what inhabits and grows at that level, and provide contrasts, so that the strands will be distinguishable in sound. For example, the top layer might move slowly and have low pitch because the trees are old, have shortish, intermittent sounds because it is the least 'solid' layer, be moderately loud and played on a tenor recorder as it sees a number of birds. Children tend to come up with well-justified and more interesting ideas than I do, but sometimes they need a lot of help at this stage, if progress to instruments is to go smoothly.

Depending on the ability and experience of the groups, working things out in sound can take quite a long time, the overall construction being based on consonant but independent repeats of ideas. In other words, although everyone plays at the same time, the five layers of sound don't begin and end repeats together, so that like the forests, it all sounds similar, but keeps changing. (I use the analogy of how easy it is to get lost there: it all looks so similar to an outsider, but obviously isn't the same.) At this stage we have performances and/or tape pieces. I am still surprised at how often the results are meditative and affecting.

The destruction

The destruction is now introduced, going through a rather simplified cycle:

1. the trees are chopped down;
2. farmers plant crops (or graze cattle — McDonalds' politics here?);
3. growth and harvest;
4. without trees the topsoil starts to be washed away by heavy rain. The annual cycle (2, 3 and 4) is repeated about four more times, (2) and (3) becoming increasingly weaker as the soil becomes thinner, until
5. the ground has become too poor to be worth using and is abandoned.

What looked so rich and fertile was a system dependent on all its parts. The cycle transfers to sound, with the different 'layer' players taking on different parts of the cycle.

The final performance is then the rainforest and its subsequent destruction. I find it interesting to note how difficult the students seem to find going back to the meditative element of work once the second part is introduced. Whether this indicates a healthy dislike of trying to repeat last week's effects this week, or whether knowing that the environment is to be destroyed makes its setting up feel less worthwhile, I don't know. Both perhaps.

Lastly, the sound is turned into pictorial scores, usually satisfyingly lively and wonderful display material.

[*Green Teacher* 11]

The healing power of listening

Do you think that when government documents and high school heads of English departments speak of 'aural skills' they mean something like this?

How often have you heard, or participated in, a conversation in which both parties are speaking but not listening?

This could be called a 'tennis ball exchange', where 'I' is the ball and the sense of self just keeps moving back and forth. Both participants are looking inward at their own needs, trying to say what they feel. Both are treating the other as a passive audience.

"Extinguishing you with the intensity of my own me-ness"

The trouble is that it doesn't work very well. Two people can't both be talkers at the same time. Someone must listen. In most normal conversations an intuitive rhythm of speaking and listening is established. I listen to you. You listen to me. A true sharing begins. But what *is* listening? The best definition I have ever heard goes something like this: listening is learning how to put your nervous system at the disposal of another.

That's an interesting idea. It suggests an attitude which is relaxed, open and receptive. For the time being at least I have laid aside my concerns and opened myself to yours. Thus one aspect of real listening has to do with our willingness to be vulnerable. That willingness can only proceed from the strength of deep self-knowledge.

There are levels of listening and listening skills. There are attitudes to listening and decisions to make about how I undertake the process. I may listen with heart or head. I may suspend all judgement or be intensely diagnostic. I may listen to the words you are using, to the implicit and explicit meanings, to the things you are not saying. With empathy and skill I may hear what you

are saying or what you are avoiding. I have to decide how to listen.
I may work to understand what you are saying but what I hear
won't be exactly what you say because I often cannot avoid
interpreting. Listening is never neutral and many meanings are
ambiguous, fluid, negotiable. Thus I may need to seek clarification,
to ask you to re-state something, to explore some fresh aspect of
the discourse we are creating. Listening is a mutual process in
which a great deal of healing can take place.

There is a phenomenology of listening. A whole world of
understanding about this mysterious and powerful process. But
the essence of it can be conveyed through a simple metaphor.

Just reflect for a moment on the data pouring into your system
through the senses of touch, sound, sight, smell and taste. Add to
this your inner awareness of who you are: your identity, biography,
feelings, your sense of purpose, your unique social position, the
dominant themes of your life. All this knowing is patterned and
rhythmic. It flows. We are each like a superb orchestra and the
music we play is the music of our own life.

Here is a key point. The music we hear is mostly our own. Because
of the way our senses work we are more real to ourselves than
others are to us. Perception is assymetrical. I can know my
experience directly, but yours reaches me as if from a great
distance. I cannot know you directly and in this fact lies the source
of much selfishness and cruelty. But I can learn to listen.
Learning to listen essentially involves actively dealing with the
'me-ness' of my experience. It involves rising far enough above

"To Echo and Celebrate that Unique Music Within You."

egotistic concerns to the point where I want to listen. At that point I can begin to consciously develop some of the many skills involved.

To return to the orchestra. I can say that in terms of my experience you are like a flute that is being played far away along some distant corridor. When my orchestra is in full swing, when I am angry, excited, anxious or dominated by some other powerful emotion or state, I simply cannot hear you. In effect, I extinguish you with the intensity of my own 'me-ness'. In order to hear the flute at all I need to learn how to damp down the orchestra, to moderate the music.

When I hear the flute I have a number of choices. I may decide that I don't like your melody. Perhaps I've heard it before and think I know it well enough to ignore the rest. I may just not be interested. And, indeed, from my point of view you may not be playing the flute very well. What, then, is my role? That depends upon the relationship between us. If you are a child I may implicitly expect you to learn my music instead of playing your own. Every parent faces that choice daily. If you are a partner I may be loving, interested, supportive . . . or indifferent. But if I want you to be yourself, if I care enough to put you first, I have another choice. To the extent that I have succeeded in shifting the centre of my being out of states of fear and limitation, away from the attachments and desires of mental-egotistic life, I can choose to moderate my melody and to change it so that it begins to support yours. Or perhaps to simply echo or celebrate that special and unique music within you. I have to be very secure to do this, very selfless to hold my melody in abeyance. Or could supporting others, really listening to others, become part of my melody?

Listening has such power it can change lives. It is an active principle that goes way beyond verbal exchanges. We can learn to listen to our feelings, to the deep wisdom of the body, to sources of knowledge and inspiration that extend far beyond any measure of personality. What else is meditation but a specialised and high-level mode of listening?

[Richard Slaughter in *Green Teacher* 11]

5: Down to earth

Earth education

If, after reading an earlier chapter, you were inspired to ask 'Where *can* we see all this wonderful experiential work on ecology, involving children as whole people in exciting discovery?' here is one of the answers.

The first ever issue of *Green Teacher* carried a major article on Earth Education, and more recently a whole issue was done as a co-production with the UK Earth Education people. Earth Education (EE) comes from the USA: the father of EE is Steve Van Matre, who comes to Britain each year to run workshops (see Chapter 8 for address).

The first extract is from *Green Teacher* No. 1, an article by Ian Duckworth, one of EE's leaders in Britain. The others are shorter quotes by Ian and other writers from the co-produced *Green Teacher* No. 12.

Some academic disciplines and teaching schemes regard part of their strength to be adherence to no values other than that of the subject itself: they maintain that their content is value free. However, at the end of our 'Special Conference', a contribution from Trevor Pinch, Lecturer in Sociology at the University of York, made clear that not only is selection of material for study a value-laden activity, but so is even defining that which we consider to be knowledge to select from. Some may then consider it refreshing that Earth Education plainly states its position, in what it terms the 'whys' of Earth education. It certainly helps us to clarify why we want to do something and that in turn helps provide the energy needed to undertake the tasks.

The whys

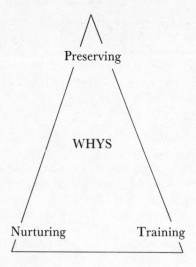

Preserving

We believe the earth as we know it is endangered by its human passengers, through:

1. soil depletion;
2. biological contamination;
3. habitat destruction
4. atmospheric pollution.

Nurturing

We believe people who have broader understandings and deeper feelings for the planet as a vessel of life are wiser and healthier and happier.

Training

We believe earth advocates are needed to serve as environmental leaders and models, and to champion the existence of earth's nonhuman passengers.

If people, young or old, are to undertake action on environmental issues they, of course, must be aware of the present, have knowledge about their role in this world and be responsible for its future. To translate all this into action they must also feel for it. They must relate to the earth and its life as a whole.

So far environmental education has failed to provide a flicker of the action witnessed recently when Bob Geldorf tapped the concern present in young people, by his Band Aid activities to alleviate the effects of famine. Action is most often initiated by feelings rather than knowledge or awareness. Young people related to those in dire distress and acted. It is the goal of Earth education to help develop this kind of productive relationship with the natural world. The components necessary to produce it are set out in the 'whats' of earth education. They help us clarify what we want to achieve. How else can you take appropriate action to effect something if you do not know what it is?

The whats

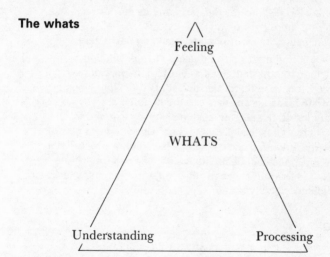

Understanding

We believe in developing in people a basic comprehension of the major ecological systems and communities of the planet:

1. the flow of energy;
2. the cycling of matter;
3. the interrelating of life;
4. the changing of forms.

Feeling

We believe in instilling in people deep and abiding emotional attachments to the earth and its life:

1. a love for the earth;
2. a kinship with all living things;
3. a reverence for natural communities;
4. a joy at being in touch with the elements.

Processing

We believe in preparing people to live more harmoniously and joyously with the earth and all its passengers, by:

1. assimilating understandings for how life works on the earth;
2. enhancing feelings for the earth and its life;
3. crafting more harmonious life-styles;
4. participating in environmental planning and action.

To achieve these ends, Earth Education has developed a methodology that has attracted a lot of attention, not least from other educators wishing to 'borrow' some of its ingenious activities. Some of the ideas encapsulated in the material are so good this is perhaps understandable, but each activity is designed to fulfil particular objectives, usually integrated with others as part of a complete programme, and the whole is carefully structured to produce a cumulative effect. The variety of Earth Education activities and the guidelines for their organisation and execution are contained in the 'ways' of Earth Education.

The ways

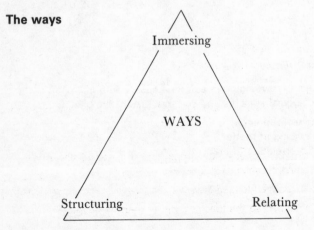

Structuring

We believe in building complete programmes with adventuresome, magical learning experiences that focus on specific outcomes.

Things to do:

1. create magical learning adventures;
2. focus on sharing and doing;
3. emphasis on 3 R's — reward, reinforce, relate;
4. model positive environmental behaviours.

Things to avoid:

1. naming and labeling;
2. talking without a focal point;
3. playing twenty questions;
4. drifting into activity entropy.

Immersing

We believe in including lots of rich first-hand contact with the natural world.

Relating

We believe in providing individuals with time to be alone in natural settings where they can reflect upon all life.

[*Green Teacher* 1]

Here is a checklist of questions to decide if a set of activities can be given the name Earth education:

- Does it tackle the basic concepts of:
  how life operates on the planet;
  the flow of energy;
  the cycling of the materials of life;
  the interrelationship of all living things with each other and with their surroundings;
  the changing of forms?
- Does it provide opportunities to use the senses and develop a personal relationship with the natural world?
- Does it introduce ideas of how we can live more lightly on Earth?
- Do the activities do the teaching rather than the leaders?

- Are the abstract ideas made concrete enough for all to understand?
- Is full participation achieved at all times?
- Do the leaders take every opportunity to reward and reinforce the learners and relate the content to everyday life?
- Do the leaders avoid playing twenty questions to get answers to questions the learners never asked?
- Do the leaders adopt a 'share and do' approach rather than the usual 'show and tell'?
- Do the leaders and activities not focus on names and naming?

[*Green Teacher* 12]

Sunship Earth

Sunship Earth is a complete five-day programme for helping kids to understand how their world functions — through seeing, smelling, tasting, touching and hearing — and to enjoy the understanding. The programme is both the concepts (the water cycle or plant succession), and the feelings — how a handful of soil looks close-up, or what a forest sounds like at dawn.

The journey starts in a strange, dimly lit room, the music beats and we are transported deep into space; moving rapidly from images of planet Earth out into the Milky Way and far out amongst distant galaxies. How vast everything seems — and how small planet Earth is when compared to the whole universe. How small, yet how full it is with things to see, touch, smell, listen and taste.

Our planet, 'Sunship Earth' (because it is powered by the energy from the sun), has been running on automatic pilot for millions of years. The problem now is that the human passengers on board our Sunship have started to tamper with the life systems and endanger not their own lives, but the lives of all their fellow passengers. Throughout the week the children will gain some understanding about how life on the Sunship functions by discovering the meaning of the formula EC–DC–IC–A.

Having crawled into a giant leaf disguised as 'chlorospies', they discover the secrets of an amazing food factory that converts sunlight energy to food. On surveying a proposed development site for new housing they learn of existing rich communities. The burial of some very special leaves in the woodland graveyard seems at first to be a sombre affair, but soon turns into a noisy birthday party.

The children get wet and dirty, they chase and are chased, they climb, hang, jump, run and sit. Indeed, learning to just sit in the natural world is an important part of the programme and we take them to some beautiful places to learn, because feeling is as important as understanding.

It is everything from 'shrinking' to get a bug's-eye view of the world to being a long-rooted plant in a drought year, from carrying leaky buckets that represent energy flow to becoming fireflies whose dance is part of the fascinating world of night. Most of all, it is learning bout how this very special planet, our'sunship', operates, and how we can both enjoy the ride and help keep the ship going on behalf of all the passengers. By the end of the week the children realise that they are just beginning their journey and that theirs is an important role in helping secure the future of planet earth.

I recommend the ride, it's well worth the risk of a speeding ticket.

[*Green Teacher* 12]

Earthwalks

Earthwalks are perhaps the best known and most widely used Earth Education programme. They are relatively easy to put together and are used by many people as an introduction to the natural world. Very often Earthwalk activities will turn up in other people's programmes — they are that good!

An Earthwalk is a special adventure in experiencing the richness and wonders of the natural world. The emphasis is on reawakening individual senses and sharpening perception.

An Earthwalk is usually from four to six activities, put together in a smooth and flowing way. The length of the entire walk is from forty five minutes to one and a quarter hours. It provides a touch of nature, a new way of looking at familiar things, and an interesting introduction to unfamiliar things too.

I have taken dozens of Earthwalks in the last few years. Many have been of mixed age groups, like the one I took a few weeks ago. . . .

I had in my diary 'Earthwalk for local Watch Group. 2.00. Bystock Woods'. I was prepared for 20+ children and as cars arrived I went to welcome them. Out of the cars climbed the adult members of the local Wildlife Trust, only two below the age of 60! My mistake, but what could I do but take them on an Earthwalk, as billed?

30 minutes later I stood back and watched these'youngsters',

some with walking sticks hanging from a handy branch, leading each other blindfolded and giggling through the woods.

[*Green Teacher* 12]

Earthkeepers

Earthkeepers is the latest Earth Education programme to be published. It is directed towards 10- to 12-year-olds and takes place partly in school and partly at the outdoor centre. The aim of Earthkeepers is, like all Earth Education programmes, to help children understand basic ecological ideas, to enjoy and to develop positive feelings about theearth and its life. They also undertake to live more 'lightly' on planet earth and to share some of the things they have learned with others — perhaps at home or at school.

Approximately two weeks before the children leave for the outdoor centre a strange map and a letter arrives in their school. They are from a character known as E.M. (pronounced em!). E.M. is already an Earthkeeper and also the 'keeper of the keys' (the keys necessary for unlocking the secrets of becoming an Earthkeeper). No one ever sees E.M. It's strange, but we always just miss her/him: the rocking chair is still rocking when we enter the room, the curtains are still moving when he/she has just left the room.

When the children arrive at the centre they enter E.M.'s lab. They find it lit by candles and full of natural sounds. There is a peaceful atmosphere and the accumulated paraphanalia of a lifetime's adventures and exploration in the natural world. During the Earthkeepers programme the children will discover four secret meanings of E.M. and they will do this by earning four different keys (K,E,Y, and S keys). To earn the K key for **knowledge** the children study four basic ecological ideas. Their E key for **experience** is gained only after they have learned that a combination of knowledge and experience of feelings provide a supporting foundation for positive environmental attitudes and action for the future. To receive the Y key for **yourself** the children must lessen their impact on the earth by pledging to follow one way for using less energy and one way for using less materials and they must deepen their feelings for the earth by pledging to complete two experiences. While it is important to be careful not to mess things up on the planet yourself, it is important to help others do the same. To receive the S key for **sharing**, the children will pledge to complete two tasks for sharing knowledge and two tasks for sharing their experience. Each key opens a padlocked box in E.M.'s lab and reveals one of the secret meanings of E.M. The first two keys are earned at the centre and last two back at school.

We have only recently started Earthkeepers at the centre, so our experience is limited. To date, however, the response of the children to the incentive of earning their own set of keys and discovering the identity of the elusive E.M. has been very positive. The teachers, too have enjoyed the synergistic nature of the programme and its completeness, with work for the 'heart and the hands' as well as for the head!

In the future more work needs to be done to share school's experiences of the Y and S tasks and I would be happy to hear from anyone with practical classroom experience of recycling and similar activities.

[*Green Teacher* 12]

Earthpark

Some years ago the education staff of the Urban Wildlife Group in Birmingham, which in 1980 was the first group of its kind in the country, had a dream. They would convert an ex-industrial canal-side site into a beautiful, magical community environmental resource. The Norman Street Project is now well advanced, and before long should be ready to fulfil its aims, which are:

- To develop an 'urban wildlife site' within the inner city to be used and enjoyed by local people, with an emphasis on community involvement at all stages.

- To develop a new and innovative educational facility that will inspire *all* groups, including professionals, interested in developing techniques in environmental education and community landscapes, as well as residents, children and all manner of visiting parties.

- To demonstrate landscape techniques for the reclamation of derelict urban sites by the establishment of natural vegetation and habitat creation.

The development of the site is following four themes: (a) to be a centre for Earth education; (b) to introduce ideas of alternative technology and resource conservation; (c) to promote play within nature, learning through discovery and experience; and (d) to involve artists with the work and promote art in the environment. These four themes are expanded below.

a. Earth education involves using the immediate landscape as a facility for developing a personal awareness of our interrelationship with the earth, and our use and abuse of it. Principles of Earth Education, as developed by Steve Van Matre and the Sunship Earth Programme, will be incorporated from the beginning of the project through design, implementation and development stages.

b. Alternative technology. The aim here is to demonstrate how the things we do, and the technology we use in our everyday lives, affect wildlife and the ecosystem.

A much broader spectrum of environmental issues and nature conservation will be looked at, focusing on simple ways in which we can save money and reduce our own environmental impact through resource conservation. Better use of natural resources such as sunshine, wind and the surrounding landscape will also be studied.

c. Play with nature. The project aims to break away from the traditional 'Nature Study Area' format, where nature can often be seen as just another classroom topic. The site will provide a setting and atmosphere for learning through imaginative play, experience and discovery, which will provide a valuable stage for developing an appreciation of the natural environment. The design will therefore incorporate hard-wearing, imaginative and robust elements.

d. Art in the environment: sculpture, mosaics and murals are all recognised as highly effective but under-used media for putting across ecological concepts. Opportunities will be made wherever possible to involve artists at various stages of the project. The site already possesses a new pair of gates, designed and made by local children in partnership with Hilary Cartmel.

The project includes the building of an advanced, passive solar design resource centre, which will itself be a 'first' in Britain. Another first will be the use of canal boats as an integral part of the project.

The group have already made a start in several different ways, so community and educational involvement is being built up during the finance-raising and building stages. Playschemes have been run, earth education holidays provided, and tree-planting schemes and recycling activities have been started with six schools.

Earthpark, and other ambitious schemes like it, deserve our admiration and support. How about starting one near you?

6: Green Craft, Design and Technology

This is the longest piece in Part Two. I decided to include it because it fits so exactly one of our six 'assumptions' in Chapter 4 about teaching green: that we want to help students design and use sustainable technologies and lifestyles. Green CDT would fill the bill exactly! Many CDT teachers are constantly looking out for new project ideas. A few suggestions, along the lines Colin Mulberg suggests below, could make a big difference. CDT (why use proper names when mysterious initials will do?) is a bit of a puzzle to many parents. Bits of it appear to be continuations of the old metalwork and woodwork, some bits of it are entirely new, and CDT as a whole can appear to mean different things at different times. What follows is a rather brutal, but minimally adequate, summary, before we get onto the main section on Green CDT, which is by Colin Mulberg. After graduating from the only UK university course in Appropriate Technology, at Warwick, he has taught, and examined CDT, from 11-year-old level to 'A'-level. He is in charge of 'A'-level design at Brentside High School, Ealing, when he is not doing an MA in Science, Technology and Society at Brunel University.

CDT, broadly, is about meeting people's needs through design. This is best understood as a process. CDT aims to enable students to identify and research problems, analysing them and finding the information required to clarify them. Next comes the ideas stage: possible solutions are refined and sifted until one is selected for the next stage. Here students produce, or make, their chosen design. Finally comes the crucial stage of evaluation — does the solution solve the problem?

The three elements of CDT can exist separately, and in the past did so. It is their combination that makes CDT a rich field, and a fertile one, whether you are using it to produce useful employees for the mega-machine or to enhance green education.

Craft skills involve the making of things: previously in wood or metal, but today it could be plastics, ceramics, textile, and soft materials.

Design is CDT's central — and educationally crucial — component. It uses the old 'technical drawing' occasionally, but the design process mentioned earlier is the key part.

Technology is the application of scientific principles to solutions to problems. There is an unfortunate assumption these days that this means high-tech, but this can be resisted.

Read on, and you'll be ready for some very interesting discussions if anyone tries to blind you with technology when talking about your child's CDT education.

A balanced CDT course has many possibilities for being green, due to the different types of activity that takes place within the subject. The first few we will look at can be easily incorporated into any CDT course.

1. Green projects

The beauty of CDT is that the design projects are totally open to choice by the teacher, and later on, by the student. The learning of skills and knowledge comes through following a design process to solve a problem; the choice of problem is not defined. Obviously, certain problems lend themselves to the teaching of certain skills and knowledge. So for example, if certain mechanical principles need to be taught in CDT: Technology, the teacher would choose a project where the likely solutions are going to involve the principles she or he wants to teach. But the *context* of the project can be varied. Though there are a number of strategies for greening CDT, this is the most obvious.

2. Following a full design process

As students complete many projects during their CDT education, they would soon get bored if all the projects were green; it must not be forgotten that in many cases their world is full of stereos, videos, computers, pop music and fashion. It is inevitable that some projects will include these areas.

But a balanced CDT course focuses on problem-solving and meeting people's needs. If this part of the design process is fully developed, CDT will be naturally people-centred, as they are the reason for designing. It is continually stressed to students that a design only succeeds if it solves the initial problem. In this respect,

CDT can be green whatever problem is chosen, if the following areas are covered in detail.

(a) Designing for the individual

Students should be encouraged to research and understand people's needs, which may be different from their own. This is especially so when designing for an unfamiliar context; for example, projects to help the infirm or disabled involve much background research.

If the problem and associated research is based around a 'green' problem, then green principles will be involved, which the student must understand to proceed through a design process. Successful projects have been:

- Anything to do with bicycles — e.g. parking stand, planning facilities.
- Design for School Nature Area.
- Insulation feasibility study (used at 'A'-level).
- Rubbish compressor.
- Can processor (removes tops/bottoms, and flattens cans for recycling).
- Jar label remover (so jars can be re-used).
- Power from play (playground equipment that generates electricity).
- Plant frost detector.
- Information posters on any green subject.

There are many more possibilities.

It is important for the teacher to have some background information, but the students can often find their own. At present it is also possible to get publicity from a green project, especially if there is the remotest possibility of the local community being affected or involved.

(b) Design for need

The difference between 'needs' and 'wants' can be made clear through a choice of projects, especially if only 'real' situations are considered. Here, the context becomes very important; designing a disco sound–light system for the sake of it is unacceptable. But designing a light warning system for deaf people may be a worthwhile project.

(c) Including 'social' factors

Students are taught to study the system that their design will fit into and so not only consider the physical thing that they are making. At a simple level, this involves the idea of the 'user' and how she or he is going to use/abuse the finished design. This links to both designing for the individual and design for need.

High-rise housing is one example. When social factors are examined, the effect of a design on society can be reviewed, as can the effects of pollution on the balance of the ecosystem. 'A'-level Design students are quite happy considering the activity of design as something that improves the 'quality of life'.

(d) Technology assessment and choice

In CDT, it is the solving of the problem that is paramount. The best technology is one that best helps to do this; it is the most 'appropriate'. This could be high technology, but is not necessarily so; for years public telephone boxes used leather straps as hinges, rather than complicated mechanisms or advanced materials.

To put this across, it is necessary to remove the 'glamour' of high technology, and return it to the status of simply being a tool. If this is coupled to the idea of designing for a complete system, including people, then the effects of design decisions can be followed through. In CDT, students must consider the technology, materials and manufacturing processes they include in a design, in a wide spectrum.

(e) Design as compromise

Students learn early on that no design solution is perfect. One of the skills they learn is how to trade off such factors as cost and performance against dissimilar factors like social effects and energy use. They realise that most designs evolve to be sold eventually, but that profit *must not* be the main consideration in a design. It is quite legitimate to recommend that a design is not produced, for one reason or another.

3. Specialist green areas

Incorporating further green elements into CDT often depends on the skill/knowledge of the teacher. For example, though it is relatively easy to understand the concept of using only natural resources, it required skill to incorporate it into a CDT project, and show how natural materials can be used in practice. Some more possibilities for green CDT are given below.

(a) Advertising/marketing

In an ideal world, marketing is used by manufacturers to find out what people want produced, and then after production advertising is used to advise customers and provide enough information so that they buy exactly what they want. It can be quite a shock for students to realise that the world does not work like this. Well-known case studies such as Coca-Cola and Levi's jeans can bring home the point that advertising creates wants and plays on psychological fears. This again reinforces the idea of 'design for need'. It is possible to link this to work in English and Media Studies.

(b) Appropriate technology

Linked to the idea of 'technological assessment and choice', appropriate technology is concerned with the concept that technology should be 'appropriate' to the situation in which it is being used. Each piece of technology must therefore satisfy the user, the society or culture in which it is being used, as well as the ecosystem. A number of pieces of technology have been developed that fit this criterion, and so have been labelled 'appropriate'; they range from alternative energy sources such as wind generators and solar heaters to whole waste recycling schemes. A familiar example of appropriate technology is the humble bicycle.

While it is easy to present a case study of a piece of appropriate technology and base CDT work around it, it is harder to teach the underlying philosophy of how to assess technology by differing criteria, and choose the most appropriate. Courses such as those run by the Centre for Alternative Technology are developing this knowledge in CDT teachers.

(c) Intermediate technology (IT)

IT is a term used to describe appropriate technology in Third World countries. The idea is to develop a range of technologies that are not high tech., but not low technology like sticks and stones. The aim is to end up somewhere between the two — intermediate technology. Projects based in the Third World easily capture students' imaginations, and seem to naturally follow on from Live Aid, disaster appeals, etc. Projects include:

- emergency shelter;
- veterinary box for India (IT Development Group project pack);
- Fuel-efficient ceramic stoves (IT Development Group project pack).

As with appropriate technology projects, IT projects need a fair bit of preparation, much of it information gathering. It must be remembered that the technical elements remain the same; it is the context that needs to be understood. The Intermediate Technology Development Group have a number of packages already prepared for CDT, and are happy to advise on the development of other projects.

Imbalances in CDT courses

An analysis of CDT tends to paint a beautiful picture, with students going out into the world to solve problems. In well-balanced courses this actually happens, with students leaving school having learnt to communicate with people and understand and appreciate their needs. They are sensitive to the environment, as they are to their own society. But they are confident that help can be given, and needs can be met.

However, not all CDT courses are like this. Some have not yet made the transition from traditional craft courses, others lack the staff or training to give the freedom and input that will make a CDT course green. A CDT course can be imbalanced for a number of reasons:

1. Craft design: older staff may be superb craftspeople, and teach very well the manipulative skills, but not do much on design,

2. Creative design: other courses may be art-based, with the creativity shown in the end product being emphasised, but with problem-solving being underplayed.

3. Trivial or prescriptive design: this situation arises if all students ever make is the traditional pencil-holders, windscreen-scrapers, etc., and/or if the work for individuals, or (more often) the whole class, is set in advance by the teacher.

4. Hardware technology: electronics, robots, etc. have a fatal fascination and often find their way into CDT departments for

ill-thought-out reasons. Because they are glossy and expensive, they get used, with emphasis being on the technology itself rather than how it can be *used* to solve real problems.

5. Industrial design: consumer design, for profit, is an important element that pupils need to meet, but they should not be given the impression that kettle-styling is what it's all about.

6. Boy-centred design: CDT can both adopt, and make worse, sexist prejudices. Girls' interests, and non-macho attitudes, must be central to course design if CDT is to be an equal opportunity subject.

7. Teaching only for GCSE: all three CDT GCSEs have very limited scope for green work, so the years from 14 to 16 could be rather barren if teachers stick too narrowly to the letter of the syllabus.

Summary

CDT is unlike other subjects at secondary level, and is gaining a unique flavour at primary level. Though problem identification and solving is a common human activity, this is the only subject that includes it as a large component. This is why green CDT can have a major effect.

The nature of CDT is particularly welcoming to a green philosophy, and using green projects will certainly educate students in such vital issues. But nationally, CDT has been slow to take green issues on board. Some departments are resisting change, and there is little training and/or support material for the interested teacher. Though the willingness is there, care must be taken to question teachers and departments to see if they have made the transition; the checklist that follows might help.

Green CDT — course checklist

These questions should show if a CDT course includes green issues. Any balanced course should appear favourable, even if green elements are not expressly included. Comments and ideal answers are given in brackets.

1. Where do projects come from?
   (From the teacher in lower years, leading to student input in later years.)

2. Are projects:

(a) Prescriptive? (Should allow different approaches/solutions.)
(b) Real? (Not imaginary.)
(c) Reflect needs (People must *need* solution.)

3. How is research and decision-making in projects conducted?
   (Some information from teacher, but most from students.)

4. Is there a balance between craft, design and technology?
   (Design is the most important, but all three should be included.)

5. How is technology used?
   (It should not dominate, but be used to solve problems.)

6. Are 'social' projects ever run?
   (At least one should be.)

7. Do teachers have an awareness of green issues?
   (If they have no awareness, then green projects are unlikely. Try asking if they have heard of certain green organisations or publications.)

8. Is the subject made attractive to girls?
   (Awareness of the problem is important, even if not many girls take the subject at GCSE.)

9. Are there any multicultural elements in the course?
   (Some schools are promoting equal opportunities, and so include projects based in different cultures, or use examples of technology from other lands.)

Finally, the big question:

10. Is there *evidence* of green teaching?
    (Look through examples of work, displays, posters, etc.)

[*Green Teacher* 14]

Intermediate technology

The following is an example of the sort of the project Colin Mulberg was referring to.

Design a Blue Cross veterinary box

Can you design a box for the 'barefoot vets' of India? It must be:

(1) large enough to take all their equipment;

(2) light enough to be easily carried;

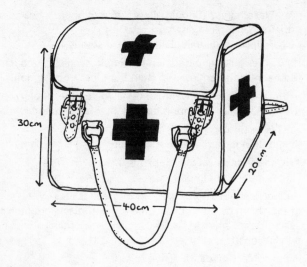

(3) sturdy enough to withstand transporting over country districts;

(4) able to offer some protection against sun and weather;

(5) be easy to make from cheap local materials;

(6) be structured to prevent breakages.

There are two sorts of Blue Cross box in use at present. Both are made in locally available materials (canvas and re-used aluminium) and both weigh nearly 1 kg when empty.

The canvas bag above, is rather like an old-fashioned school satchel. Inside the contents get all jumbled together, bottles sometimes get broken, and equipment is not easy to find.

The aluminium case shown opposite was designed to prevent the problem of spillage and breakage. There is an internal metal partition to help keep bottles upright, and a metal compartment in the lid to hold the deshi's record book. However, the metal handle is very uncomfortable and like the bag, the box is quite heavy.

[Intermediate Technology Department Group]

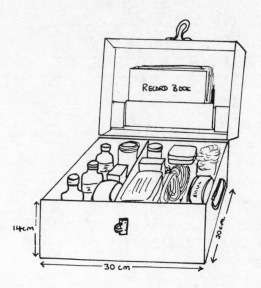

Windy?

You thought wind power technology was out of reach of your 10-year-olds? Too ambitious for your 14-year-olds? At the Centre for Alternative Technology children of all ages from 7 to 57 (and older!) have had great fun, and learned a lot — both about the science of electricity and about the design process — by using plans such as these shown in Figure 4 overleaf. They originate with the education publications of the US Department of Energy. Books full of such ideas are available by mail order from the bookshop at the Centre for Alternative Technology.

Solar hot-dogs

How often do you get to test your educational progress by eating it? OK, yes, cookery lessons, but technology? Primary schoolchildren in several schools have already combined gastronomy (of a sort) with technology using the following idea.

WHAT IS THE BEST ANGLE AT WHICH TO SET THE BLADES OF A PROPELLER TO MAKE ELECTRICITY?

MATERIALS:

Balsa wood, 1.6mm thick piece

Balsa wood, 12.5mm thick piece

⎫ *Use for making all propellers in Activities 8 and 9*

Small 1 1/2 volt DC motor

100 ohm, 1/2 watt resistor

⎫ *hobby/electronics shop*

Voltmeter, 0-2 volts *(Government stores)*

Powerful 2-or 3-speed room fan *(different fans give different results — experiment with more than one)*

Fine hacksaw blade, glue

Teacher's discretion! → Single-edged razor blade

Small nail and hammer or drill

Plastic insulated hookup wire, about 30cm

Plastic model airplane propeller *Note: The balsa propellers you make below do not have an aerofoil shape — the model aeroplane propeller does.*

Build a propeller like this:

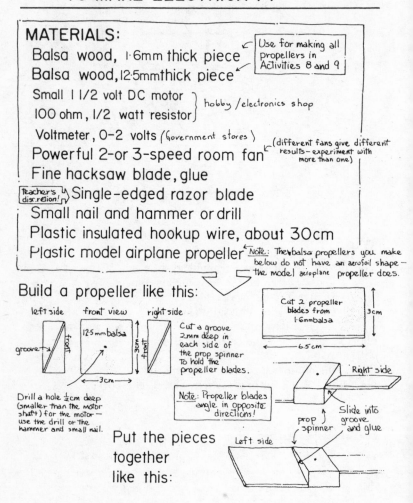

left side   front view   right side

12.5mm balsa

3cm

front

groove →

Drill a hole ½cm deep (smaller than the motor shaft) for the motor — use the drill or the hammer and small nail.

Cut a groove 2mm deep in each side of the prop spinner to hold the propeller blades.

Cut 2 propeller blades from 1.6mm balsa

3cm

6.5cm

Note: Propeller blades angle in opposite directions!

Right side

prop spinner

Slide into groove and glue

Left side

Put the pieces together like this:

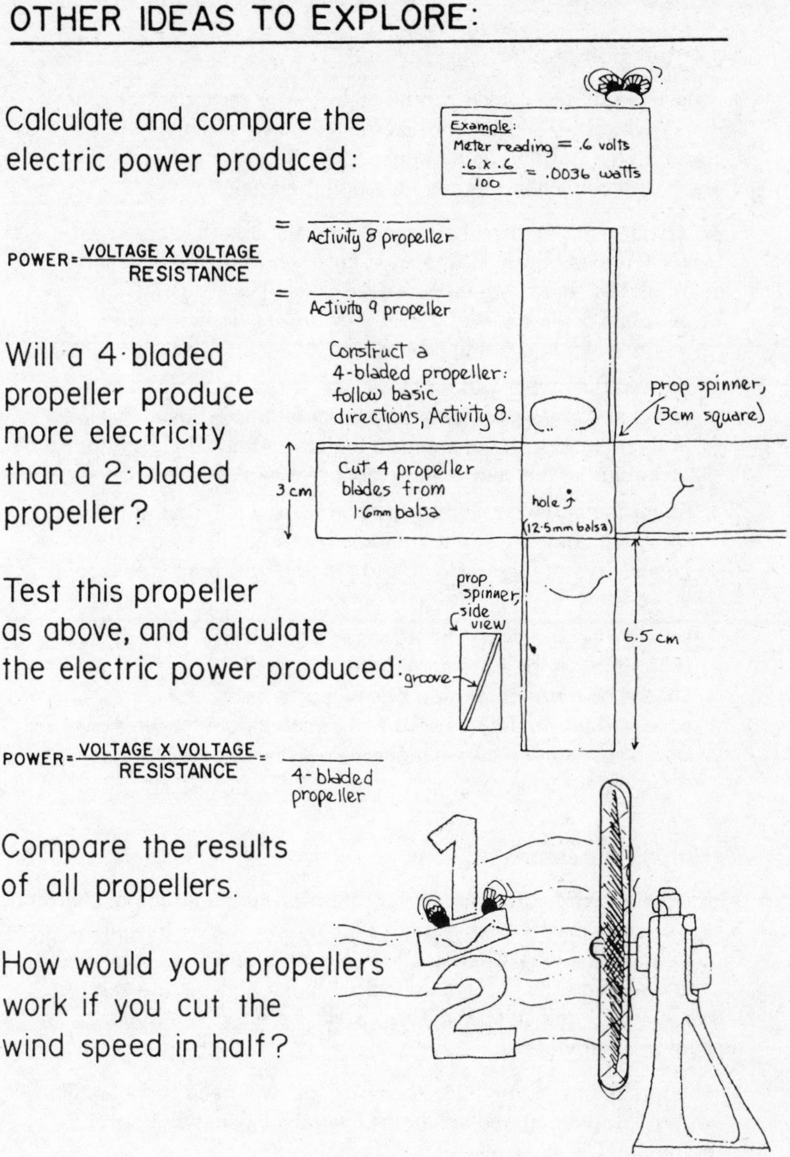
OTHER IDEAS TO EXPLORE:

Calculate and compare the electric power produced:

$$\text{POWER} = \frac{\text{VOLTAGE X VOLTAGE}}{\text{RESISTANCE}} = \underline{\qquad}\ \text{Activity 8 propeller}$$

$$= \underline{\qquad}\ \text{Activity 9 propeller}$$

Will a 4-bladed propeller produce more electricity than a 2-bladed propeller?

Test this propeller as above, and calculate the electric power produced:

$$\text{POWER} = \frac{\text{VOLTAGE X VOLTAGE}}{\text{RESISTANCE}} = \underline{\qquad}\ \text{4-bladed propeller}$$

Compare the results of all propellers.

How would your propellers work if you cut the wind speed in half?

Example:
Meter reading = .6 volts
.6 x .6 / 100 = .0036 watts
Construct a 4-bladed propeller: follow basic directions, Activity 8.
prop spinner, (3cm square)
3 cm
Cut 4 propeller blades from 1·6mm balsa
hole
(12·5mm balsa)
prop spinner, side view
groove
6.5 cm
1
2

Figure 4: Part of plans for a wind generator. From Green Teacher 5.

Solar hot dog cooker

A reflective hot dog cooker can be built from a cardboard box, tin foil and posterboard. Sunlight hits the reflective surface and focuses on the hot dog held in the centre. Students can work in pairs, or individually if there are enough materials.

1. Select a long narrow box; the longer the box the more heat collection is possible. Choose a focal length between 5 and 10 inches, and design a parabolic curve (see below). One template could be used for all the cookers. Trace the curve on the open end of the box so that it is centred and straight.

2. Cut out the curve with a utility knife. Stress the importance of being exact. Measure and cut a piece of posterboard that will fit flush against the opening to the box. Attach this with tape, beginning at the centre and working toward the edges.

3. Cover the curve with white glue and apply aluminium foil, shiny side out. Start in the middle and smooth toward the edges. Try not to wrinkle or fold the foil; you want it as smooth as possible.

4. Use two scraps of cardboard taped to each side as supports. Using the sun or a projector light, test the focal point. There should be a bright spot on the supports where light is concentrated; mark this spot and punch a hole for the skewer. Use a section of a coat hanger from which the paint has been removed for a skewer.

Designing a parabola

A parabolic curve is the only shape that can bring light into a sharp focus. Circular curves yield a diffuse focus, which may be suitable for some applications. Choose a focal length that will be convenient for the size of device you are building. Remember that the shorter the focal length the steeper the curve. Here are two methods for designing a parabola:

1. The mathematical method. Your students will need to be familiar with point plotting and solving for variables using algebra. The equation is:

$$x^2 = 4cy,$$

where c is the desired focal length. Plug in a series of x values, solve for y, and plot graphically.

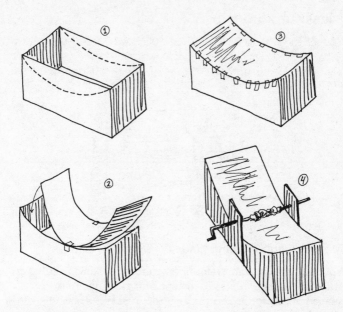

2. The parabolic shape can be determined using a T square, nail and paper. Draw a line on the top of the paper 2″ from the top and bisect this with a perpendicular. Drive a nail into the perpendicular at the desired focal length. Place the short end of the square (the tongue) against the base line and keep the body of the square in contact with the nail. Draw a line along the edge of the tongue. Making sure that the body touches the nail and the corner of the square touches the base line, move the square a few degrees at a time. Mark along the tongue after each move until the desired diameter is reached. The lines have inscribed a parabolic shape which can be duplicated on the other side or folded in half to produce a mirror image.

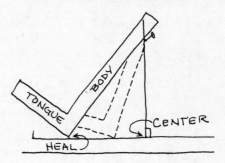

Messing about in the water

One of the resources for teachers being published about now by Intermediate Technology is about small-scale hydroelectricity, aimed at older students. Very good too, but here are one or two ideas to try with younger ones (at home even?).

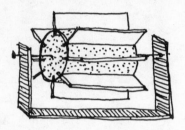

Moving water, moving blades

You can make a small water turbine model by taping cardboard strips on a cork. Put pins in the ends for axles and make a U-shaped holder for it. You can also slip metal or plastic fins into slits made in the cork. This will turn as fast as the water stream is moving, so generally turbines have high-speed jets directed towards them.

An overshot waterwheel

This model is like the old waterwheels used for grinding grain or running machines. Great power and slow speed were needed to turn the heavy grinding stones at an even speed. This device could use a relatively small stream. It is the weight of the water in the buckets that causes the wheel to overbalance and turn. You can equip your wheel with a string and bucket and find out how much weight the mechanism can lift.

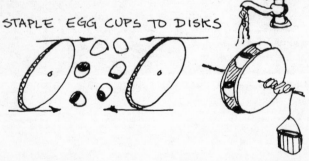

STAPLE EGG CUPS TO DISKS

And some variations on the waterwheel theme....

To make a different model of an overshot wheel, follow these steps:

1. Cut two round pieces of cardboard of diameter 8 cm.

2. Draw a circle of diameter 4 cm and glue a strip of cardboard 12.5 cm × 2 cm on the circumference of this inner circle (use contact cement).

3. Cut eight strips of cardboard 2 cm × 3 cm; glue these as vanes as shown at an angle, and glue the other circular piece (step 1) onto this to complete the wheel.

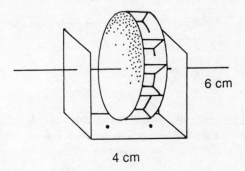

6 cm

4 cm

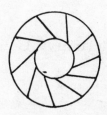

4. Make an axle for the wheel using a 6 cm piece of coat hanger wire. Glue the axle to the wheel.

5. Use a piece of wood 18 cm × 5 cm × 2 cm as the base.

6. Support the ends of the axle of the wheel in holes drilled about 1 cm from the ends of a piece of cardboard 16 cm long × 2 cm wide, and bend as shown.

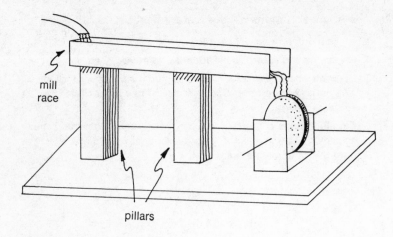

mill race

pillars

7. Fix this assembly at one end of the base using two short nails.

8. Use a plastic tooth brush box as the mill race by cutting off one end of it and gluing it on top of two pieces of wood glued to the base as pillars. One pillar should be about 1 cm shorter than the other so that the mill race will slightly slope towards the top of the wheel but not touch it.

[*Green Teacher* 5]

Centre for Alternative Technology (CAT): connections

The Quarry, as the place is affectionately known, since it occupies what was a slate quarry and slate waste tip, is a very special place. Over the last few years very large numbers of young people, and teachers, have come for a short stay and then returned to school or college informed, enlightened and inspired.

It is, physically, a magical place, and this helps a lot. And it is significant that people see things at the Quarry that they don't see elsewhere. But much more important is the way the founders of the place, and those who have followed, convey a sense of holism. At a recent 'where are we going?' meeting the staff reaffirmed that this was at the core of their work.

No wonder so many school students, when asked in discussions what is their main impression of their experience at CAT, reply with words to the effect of 'it's all connected together, isn't it?'

Learning by experience

The Centre is an exceptionally valuable place in which to conduct the residential section of educational and training courses. GCSE and A level Technology. Science and Geography groups.

We have to turn away more groups than we can accommodate, and with the rise in demand for residential work we have decided to follow up on a particularly good idea.

Two cabins are being built this autumn (1989), each to accommodate 18 people in four rooms of four bunks and 2 single rooms. Each cabin will:

- be supplied with energy from renewable sources: photovoltaics, wind-generator and water turbine for electricity with the requisite battery storage system and monitoring and control equipment, hot water from solar collectors and woodburning stove.
- have its water supply from a standpipe some distance away.
- dispose of its waste — human and vegetable – in organically ecological ways.
- contain a cooker for self-catering.
- be looked after by a resident tutor-warden, who will be on hand to assist group leaders in both domestic and educational matters.

Therefore, young people staying in the cabins will learn experientially about the question "What is the impact, on the earth, of a week in my life?"

They will learn in the most practical ways possible about renewable energy supply and storage. If they want power for the radio, there are the aerogenerator, the photovoltaics and the water turbines to be checked and the batteries and invertor to be monitored. If they want warm water the solar collectors and/or woodstove must be dealt with. If the water supply is running low, new supplies must be fetched. They will see how the toilets contribute (in a no-smell way!) to the composting process, and each group will make at least nominal contribution to food-growing work in the nearby organic plots.

Figure 5 (overleaf): Map of Centre for Alternative Technology site. From CAT visiguide.

Dunlite Aerogenerator

'Suburban' Vegetable Garden

Energy Saving House

Maze

Picnic Area

'Urban Garden

Exhibition

Solar Roof

Heat s

Community House

Solar Energy

Solar Water Heating

Organic Garden

Bees

Solar Electric

Wind Power

Compost Toilets

Fish Pond

Smallh

Concentrating Solar Collectors

up from car park

Solar Steam Engine

Reception

Electric Truck

15 kW Polenko on nearby hill

Introduction to Alternative Technology

Toilets

Solar Wall

Insulated Cottages

Biofuels Display

Forge

Energy in the Home

aterwheel

Water Turbines

Water Power

Reservoir

draulic Ram

5 kW Elektro

700 W DIY Cretan

200 W Winco

Aerotron

3 kW Catenary

Centre for Alternative Technology

MACHYNLLETH, POWYS, WALES.

Access to use of the cabins will be via the purchase, in advance, of 'time shares'. These will be available to TVEI Centres, schools, colleges, universities, company training departments, local authorities and voluntary organizations. Payment for a 'cabin-week' will cover exclusive use of the cabin from Sunday morning to Saturday noon, the services of the resident tutor-warden, and free access to the Centre at any time during opening hours (worth £1.00 per school student, and £1.50 FE or HE, per visit, at 1989 prices).

The cost works out at £4 or £5 per person per night, according to time of year.

Residential alternative technology

You may be told that alternative technology is too different, or too ambitious, a topic to tackle seriously with young people. Issue 1 of *Green Teacher*, in October 1986, contained the story below. Graham McDonald and Dr Peter Craig, at the Ballater Field Study Centre in Aberdeenshire, have further developed the course described, emphasising problem-solving. Students now emerge with a diploma in applied science.

Alternative technology — an LEA residential course

This September saw the first experience of the Ballater Field Study Centre residential course, 'Alternative Technology'. The week-long, 40-hour module forms part of a National Certificate of Science qualification. A pretty inspiring way of using residential facilities with young people. . . .

Course description

The aim of the course is to introduce students to the applied science of renewable energy systems and equipments, including solar collectors, aerogenerators and microhydroelectric generators. The course will explore the basic physics of these systems and also some of the economic, social and environmental issues associated with renewable energy. The course will be heavily practical in nature and will engage students in a range of interesting and demanding problem-solving projects in a variety of settings.

Certification

The course is registered with SCOTVEC as an Applied Science 3 Module (40 hours). Students who satisfactorily achieve the course learning outcomes will be awarded the appropriate National Certificate. Preferred entry level is Standard Grade Science at 4 on a pass in SCE 'O' Grade Science or Physics.

Accommodation

The course will be based at Ballater Field Centre, with residential accommodation provided at recently refurbished Morrone Lodge, Braemar.

[*Green Teacher* 1]

7: Approaching holism

Holistic infant teaching

Some of our 5- to 7-year-olds really are the heirs of the centuries-old progressive/holistic tradition. Hazel Waddup is head of an infants' school in Sussex.

> The near is our room, our fellows, the environment is the outcome of ourselves. It is the close-at-hand relationships. You cannot bring order to the world without bringing order to yourself.
> *Krishnamurti on Education*

At a recent conference discussing what might be the main principles of holistic education, be it called transpersonal, 'integratif' or in this case holistic, we were all open to some central issues. I decided to examine these issues in the context of the school where I work, in order to begin a dialogue for those teachers within all schools who wish or who have a holistic approach.

As we are thinking about the whole person in their whole setting, a good starting point may be the centre of a building or set of buildings, as a focus for considering the total landscape. There needs to be a commitment to one's own landscape both in its present and historical sense. I decided to start a garden in the centre of the school, a garden of herbs and wild flowers that create a quiet sanctuary and provide food for the mini-wildlife that it sustains.

Six years on, there is a place for quiet reflection, and a place for children to draw *in situ* seedheads and pond plants, a place to let go of butterflies and moths that we have bred, a place to gather and return small mini-beasts that have been examined in the classroom. It means there are always plants in various stages of evolution to provide the focus for the detailed drawings that give us pleasure and are greatly admired by visitors. By smelling, handling and drawing plants, gathering seeds, making *pot pourri* and pressing and planting flowers, children can begin to understand the contribution that plants make to our well-being via medicines, food and shelter, as well as having a spiritual significance. I am always mindful of the fact that many monks and nuns planted flowers and herbs as prayers. As wagtails live on this site, we have chosen one as our emblem on sweatshirts and notepaper. Soon we will begin, with parents' help, to develop another section of the garden to encourage more birds and butterflies.

Historically this part of the downs was used for sheep, so this year, through drama, we are exploring the role of sheep both in Biblical times and then using songs and stories from local shepherds, constructing with the children the imagined year-long cycle of family life on the downs at the turn of the century. It is this attention to landscape that gives a sense of ownership and commits the teacher to helping children gain knowledge of the flowers, trees and birds on this site. When the school vixen was found dead, she was duly buried along with other pets. Children need to understand that animals are part of the life and death of their own loved pet at home. Our own landscape at school forms a framework for working with some 250 children, from 4 to 7 years old, in as direct a way as possible, bearing in mind that many teachers share the concern that so many of this generation of children seem cut off from the earth.

Each year, through life-themes that include the elements, the seasons, personal development and scientific awareness, children learn in as tangible a way as possible. It is absurd to teach young children concepts of air, water and earth using videos and slides when they can experience them first hand by making gardens, playing with water in all different ways, throwing up parachutes and flying kites. Flag festivals help us to celebrate and show our concern for the planet. Each child designs a flag to represent a natural element that they wish to preserve.

At the conference I mentioned at the beginning of this article, our group agreed that holistic education should have a spiritual base, not necessarily from one belief system but drawing on universals and the best from all religious practices and systems. As a Buddhist with a Christian background, I encourage prayer and quiet reflection, and the use of the best stories and music from all cultures, eastern and western, to give a child a sense of place. Children need to discover for themselves why religious practices play such a large part in some people's lives, and how much of our art, literature, music has a religious significance. Holistic education in this country needs to have its own culture base, so we turn to mediaeval music, Celtic patterns, circle dancing and simple instruments and voice work to create our own celebrations as well

as traditional festivals. From among the parents we are discovering
a group of women who play recorders, piano and percussion and
they join us in our assemblies and support our arts curriculum.
Parents who come and help voluntarily in schools have many gifts
and skills to share: music, art, word-processing, writing etc.

Respect for the body comes high on the list, helping children to
understand from an early age their body structure. They can learn
parts of the body from X-rays, skeletons, body games, and
investigating healthy food. Work on the positive aspects of the
body should take precedence over playing hospitals, which can
focus on disease rather than health. Children can learn to
understand mobility and handicaps by, say, making wheelchairs for
'disabled' teddies etc. from constructional toys. Learning to design
and construct vehicles, buildings, bridges, that can empower and
facilitate other people both in our own and other cultures is a
valuable use of energy and an introduction to simple technology.
All our cooking is planned to help children make informed and
healthy choices, introducing them to wholefoods, a variety of fruits
and vegetables, and to sharing food with others. Even at parties
we avoid commercial foods that abound in additives and
colourants, and encourage children to taste natural fruit juices.
(This also has a beneficial effect on behaviour on such days). Bread
is baked at harvest times to cut up and be shared in the classes,
as a basis for beginning to understand world inter-dependence on
food. Older children experiment with spices for Indian and Chinese
food, and try out yams, pineapples and mangoes. Chapatis, chollas
and hot cross buns are cooked for festivals. Artefacts and masks
are collected and carefully made to use for drama, religious
education and art.

> Some materials and objects often satisfy unclassifiable
> cravings in many a child.
> *An Experiment in Education*, by Sybil Marshall

Festivals of lights, using dance from different countries, help to
alleviate the darkness of winter.

Empowering the body is important through voice, movement and
drama, working in groups and circles, learning to move carefully
and to respect each other's bodies. Sculptures and trust games
form an important part of this process, using what we call 'worthy'
themes. We have worked on *Jonathan Livingstone Seagull*, on parts
of *Watership Down*, on Japanese and stories from other cultures,

and on Biblical themes, both Old and New Testament. Stories about tribes and villages dealing with food and water shortages, and stories about animals such as in *Watership Down* and *The Mouse and His Child*, represent aspects of conservation and attitudes to the planet earth.

Drama is a vehicle for learning to listen, to take turns, to respect others' views and probably a good time in the school day to focus on breathing, control of body movements and respect for the other people's space and person. This work can transfer across the curriculum into group behaviour in the classroom and corridor. We try to choose themes that are gender-friendly and that add to our global literacy.

When computers were introduced into primary education, my view was rather 'Luddite'. Now we find that they give children opportunities to access and organise information quickly, to practise time-consuming skills like spelling and tables, but that they can also be used in a creative way to make and edit stories and scripts. Some of the negative aspects of TV are avoided here — we do not encourage children to write about TV programmes they have seen.

Because this is not rewarded we have noticed some children constructing elaborate games in the playground round stories they have read. A home/school reading programme links parents and school in the pursuit of reading for enjoyment and sharing. We recently were involved in making a video on 'Constructional Toys' and parents, staff and children all became part of the 'construction' of the film, sharing expertise with the camera crew, taking ownership of the project.

One of the planks of holistic education is surely empowerment, particularly in liberating the feminine, feeling side of our nature to provide a balance to the left-brain dominance of the system. Children and adults need to gain confidence by working in groups, using each other as what Stephen Rowland calls 'reflective agents', encouraging each other to take risks, and taking some responsibility for their own learning. Dependence is to be discouraged and inter-dependence sought. Children learn to take turns in leadership, to take up space with ideas and bodies and to act in a respectful non-violent way towards each other. This assumes that process mirrors process, that staff and other adults will be prepared to learn group skills of writing and planning together, working in clusters on certain curriculum areas, supporting and encouraging each other to take risks. Management styles and staff development all come

under scrutiny, as part of each cycle. To provide a learning
environment where both collaborative and individual skills are
nurtured, as well as personal development requires patience,
energy and commitment. Then we can begin to tackle 'the simple
act of walking the earth like brothers and sisters' (Martin Luther
King).

[*Green Teacher*]

Conservation visualisation

Poppy Green contributed this piece. She runs the *New Education
Directory* (see 'Resources').

We are going on an adventure. Close your eyes and listen to your
quiet breathing. Now you can hear the soft murmur of the sea and
you can feel the sand between your toes. You are sitting on the
silver sand looking out to sea. In the distance you can seen an
island. Wouldn't it be fun to go there? You wonder how you could
get over the water. The sky grows dark and you feel afraid. What
is it that's darkening the sun?

It's a giant seagull which flies down and lands beside you. 'Would
you like to ride on my back?' asks the seagull. So you get on the
seagull's back and hold on tight as you soar up into the blue sky.
Now you can see the silver sand far below and the sea with waves
white-crested like sea-horses and the island with its tall mountain
is getting nearer. Now the island is below you and the seagull
swoops gently down and rests on the beach of the island. You jump
off and watch the seagull take off and you wave as it flies away.

Now you look ahead and see a cave in the rocks up the beach
and go towards it. The cave is dark and cool. You go inside out of
the bright sunshine and walk along a damp passage. A shaft of
light shines from above and you see something on the floor among
the rocks. You look at it for some time and then leave it there for
it belongs to the cave.

You walk along the passage towards the light you can see at the
end. You come out in a beautiful, cool, green forest. The air is
humming with life. You can hear the birds in the trees. You walk
up a steep path through the tall trees that tower above you. A
special tree has branches low down and it's easy to climb. There's
a hole in the tree trunk and you can see something inside. You

look at it for some time but you leave it there because it belongs to the forest.

You climb down the tree and walk on up the steep mountain path. You climb to the very top and feel the sun on your face as you gaze down and out and around you at the wondrous view. A tumbling rock disturbs you and you look in the direction of the noise and see an animal staring at you. You spend some time with the animal but you leave it there because it belongs to the mountain.

You run down the mountain side, the wind in your face until you reach a lake at the end of the rocks. You cup the water in your hands and splash your face. Then you see something in the water below and reach to touch it. You spend some time looking at it but you leave it there because it belongs to the lake.

You run all the way back to the sand and as you arrive the seagull flies down to take you back. You climb onto its soft feathers and as it flies up you watch the island with its mountain get smaller and smaller. You can see the waves below, white crested like sea-horses and you see the silver sand getting closer, closer as the seagull wheels down and gently lands.

You climb down and thank it for helping you. The seagull gives you a box. 'This is for you', says the seagull. 'Don't open it till I've flown away.'

You watch the seagull fly and wave goodbye. 'Thank you again seagull' you cry. Then you sit on the silver sand and listen to the waves and feel the sand between your toes.

When you are ready open your eyes.

The seagull has flown away so now — open the box. Look at what is inside.

What did you find in the cave?
What did you find in the forest?
What did you find on the mountain?
What did you find in the lake?
What is in the box?

[*Green Teacher* 13]

Play for Life

Play for Life are a national voluntary organisation formed to encourage fresh thinking about the play experience of children of all ages. It aims to develop co-operation between parents, educators and the toy industry in promoting life-affirming play-things. It started in response to two areas of concern regarding:

- The influence of many games and toys that promote violent attitudes leading to aggressive and warlike behaviour and those encouraging intense competition;
- The dearth of toys offering real play potential.

Play for Life look for toys, games and hobbies that help chidren to develop a love of life through the opportunities they provide for fun, imagination, wonder, adventure, co-operation and new skills. They also seek to introduce playthings that promote an understanding and appreciation between the sexes and different cultural and racial groups.

Adults are encouraged to think about the real play needs of children, especially in the light of the kind of world in which they are growing up. Play for Life provide resource material and information, mount exhibitions, give talks and workshops, hold conferences and publish a newsletter. They research the toy market and publish the *Guide to Playthings for Life*, listing and commenting on playthings in keeping with their criteria.

The founding sponsors were the Green Party, the Peace Pledge Union, Quaker Peace and Service, and Traidcraft Educational Foundation. There are links with many other bodies, toy producers and interested individuals both in the UK and abroad.

Learning Through Action

Learning Through Action is the name of a company in Berkshire that produces educational programmes for school children; it is also the title of a diploma course for seconded teachers, but above all it is an excitiving new concept in education. It started in 1979 with honours elective courses taught by Annette Cotterill, then a senior lecturer in drama at Bulmershe College of Higher Education in Reading. It became clear that a teaching method that used drama and role-play and involved the children in active participation, aroused and sustained their interest in a topic to an extent that far exceeded other approaches.

Soon, part-time DES inservice courses were established, to train teachers in these methods, and in 1984 a full-time company, employing young, newly trained teachers, was founded, under the name of Learning Through Action, to take programmes into Berkshire schools. This led to the establishment, two years later, of one-year, full-time diploma courses for seconded teachers.

The visiting team of teachers-in-training work both in and out of role with a group of thirty to forty children and create, with them, another country, a different historical period or simply new surroundings. The children explore this environment and the artefacts they find and soon begin to relate to the people who live there and to the problems that they encounter. The emphasis of a programme is on discovery by experience and during a session all the children are actively participating, whether learning practical skills, assessing situations and making decisions, or developing their ability in language and communication.

A programme is designed, not as an isolated event, but as the stimulus to a sustained period of follow-up work on the topic. The teachers' resource pack which accompanies the programme is full of information and ideas, so that teachers can follow up the programme in a wide variety of ways.

Teachers who wish to apply for the course may come from any category of school and will learn to work with all age and ability groups. A drama background or theatre skills are not necessary as they will be developed during the course. Essential qualifications are good communication and a flexible attitude to educational ideas.

Future years will see both full and part-time courses for the training of teachers, combined with the continuing supply of this service to children in Berkshire and beyond. The group is constantly in demand to demonstrate at conferences, while many museums and organisations, including the Commonwealth Institute and the Science Museum, are realising the potential of this type of work and requesting residencies. It is also hoped in future to work with groups of students from overseas.

The aim is to make available to all teachers a method of breaking down barriers in education and in the world outside, encouraging sharing between teachers and children. It is also to implement a way of teaching through which knowledge, information and understanding are equally accessible to children of all levels of ability. In the years ahead it is hoped that the work will be extended far beyond Berkshire, reaching many more children and enhancing the skills of an increasing number of teachers.

Children's Comments

'We even missed playtime and it didn't matter because we played and learned at the same time.'

Spital First School

'This morning . . . everyone told each other about what we did in our groups. I wish you would come again before we leave school.'

Julie, Willow Bank Junior School

'You really made my afternoon the best one for ages.'

Paul, Willow Bank Junior School

'The people were good in the way that they acted as if they were learning as well, even though they were teaching us.'

Leo, Altwood School

'The reason why I liked it is because it is so different from the normal things we do at school.'

Wayne, Altwood School

'She had lots of props which we were allowed to use, which we all thought was brilliant.'

Group letter, James Elliman School

Let's Co-operate

Let's Co-operate by Mildred Masheder, a book for parents and teachers, is now a legend, into its fifth edition only three years after being published by the Peace Education Project. Her collection of over 300 co-operative games and sports, *Let's Play Together*, followed from Green Print in 1989.

Spiritual values

There are now many instances of young children meditating at home or in school. To most Westerners this seems alien to their culture, yet it is not so far removed from all of the other creative experiences we have described in that it reaches down to the inner self from where much of our creative inspiration flows.

The meditation or relaxation can be a guided fantasy or concentration on one concept such as joy. Children can close their eyes and enter into their inner minds, putting away the many thoughts that assail all of us all of the time. The atmosphere is peaceful, with some music to begin with and perhaps lighted candles; then an adult could begin to guide them in deep breathing; they could breathe in lovely feelings of peace and happiness and breathe out all the nasty thoughts. Gradually they are full of joy and happiness, they are overflowing with it so that they can spare some for someone else, someone sitting near them. With still more they can give it to all the family or all the class, then to the people living near them or the whole school, then extending to the village or town, to the whole country, the whole world, and finally the universe with its myriads of suns!

What has been amazing is that after this five- to ten-minute concentration children can produce extraordinary art, unlike anything they have ever done before; the pictures have a radiance and beauty that reflect something that has taken place within them.

[*Let's Co-operate*, by Mildred Masheder]

(6a)

(6b)

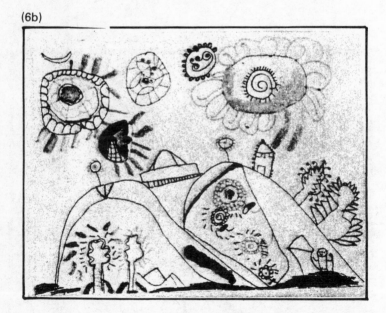

Fig. 6: Examples of children's paintings after meditation. From Masheder, Mildred, Let's Co-operate.

8: Junior recycling

Recycling drama

Exciting work does go on in schools on rubbish and recycling —
not immediately inspiring subjects. Karen Coulthard led a workshop at the 'Global Futures' conference on drama with 8- to 9-
year-olds. . . .

Drama is an excellent medium for allowing children to share and
explore ideas; it enables them to clarify the knowledge they already
have while giving the teacher the opportunity to see, not only what
they know, but where the gaps in their learning are. The following
activities use drama to explore aspects of recycling and are
designed for work with top juniors as part of a project on this
theme. All the activities can be carried out in the classroom, hall
space is not necessary. Although the work is set out as three
lessons, the children may need more time to become involved in
the activities; this is particularly important to bear in mind if
children have had little or no experience of using the medium.

Activity 1: creating a recycling machine

In groups of four or five ask the children to create an imaginary
recycling machine that they can demonstrate to the rest of the
class. This may involve any material they like (even though in
practical terms it may not be a resource that can be recycled).

When the children have discussed and planned their machine
they must find a way of 'showing' it. This could be with the children
either becoming parts of the machine, becoming the people that
operate it, or both. They should consider particular issues such as
how big the machine should be, how many different stages are
necessary, and how many people are needed to operate it.

When the children show their work it is important that the rest
of the class are encouraged to watch carefully and then ask
questions and comment on what they have seen. The group

'showing' can be questioned on their machines, their knowledge
of the resource being recycled and on how they reached their
decisions as a group. (Initially the teacher may have to 'model' this
type of questioning if the children are new to working in this way.)
At this stage observers can also contribute knowledge they may
have on the resource being considered so that a general sharing of
information takes place. As a follow-up to this the chiildren can do
a diagram of the machine, incorporating into this speculation as to
how the whole recycling process may work.

Of course, the machine the children design may not be at all
realistic and may involve a process that would be totally out of the
question — an example of this is a group that I worked with that
decided to recycle plastic bottles into plastic felt-pen cases — but
the children will have had the opportunity to begin to realise what
recycling a material would involve. As a follow-up, realistic
examples of recycling can be given, which should then have more
meaning. Questions such as 'Can plastic be recycled?' can lead
children into researching the issue to discover what is practical.
From speculation on an imaginary level children can question their
own knowledge and build on this. Follow-up activities in other
curriculum areas can be introduced to extend children's thinking
(see *Green Teacher* Issue 7).

Activity 2: use of role play/selling the idea of recycling

Like the mime used above, role play is another useful drama
strategy to use in the classroom. By adopting a role we are asking
children to imagine that they are either another person or
themselves in a different or imaginary situation. It is important to
remember that going into role is primarily a thinking activity, it
does not demand that children put on a strange voice or move in
a different way, they are not asked to 'perform' as such but to
simply imagine what they would do in the situation presented.

Once children have gathered information concerning recycling
that can or is happening at the present time they can use that
information in role. For the following activity the children are asked
to imagine that they are responsible for promoting a certain type
of recycling, and in small groups decide how they are going to try
and persuade others to support or market their project. For this
they will need to research information concerning recycling that
they can use from packs such as *Recycling: The Way Forward*
published by Friends of the Earth. If necessary this information can

be presented on cards written by the teacher at an appropriate level for the children.

The task for each group is to gather the information they think necessary and to decide how to use this in order to justify that aspect of recycling. In role they must represent someone involved in the process they are supporting. For example, children promoting glass recycling may be either someone who controls bottle banks, the manager of a cullet firm, a researcher involved in the process, a representative of a drinks firm etc. Once children have had the opportunity to plan how they are going to 'sell' or promote their recycling resource they present this to the rest of the class. Once again the children should be encouraged to question each group as they present their information, but this time the group presenting should stay in role to answer questions. As a preparation for this the children should be asked to imagine how the person they are representing in role would offer information and respond to the questioning.

As a final part of this activity the children should be encouraged to reflect on and discuss the information that arises and any difficulties they found in carrying out the task. Once again, gaps in the children's knowledge may be revealed which could involve further research and investigation.

Activity 3: looking at the issue from a local viewpoint

As a further task the children can be encouraged to consider the views of people living in the local community and how they would respond to the idea of recycling facilities being set up in the area. Children need to be aware of what is already available in their own area and any problems this may cause. (The issue of bottle banks posed two problems to the children I worked with. One was that the nearest was quite a long walk away, the other was the fact that they were not emptied on a regular basis, which meant bottles were dumped around the containers once they were full). All this information can be incorporated into a role play that enables the children to consider what would be desirable and practical for their area.

For this activity the children are asked to go into role as someone living in the area. They could be an elderly person, a member of a family living in a high rise block, a shopkeeper, a road-sweeper, etc. Either in groups of five or six or as a whole class the children have to imagine that they are at a meeting of a local community group discussing the proposal that recycling facilities be introduced into the area. Issues to be raised can include where would facilities be situated, which would be most practical, would it be better to support the recycling of one or many different resources. Doing this activity in role enables individuals to argue against all proposals (children representing this group could be agreed before the role play begins), which would demand that children arguing for recycling have clear and precise reasons for adopting any scheme, and to realise that it is not an easy thing to introduce such schemes without problems or criticism from certain groups of people.

As a preparation for the role play, each individual could be given a little time to consider where this person lived, how they would be affected by the proposals and what their attitude would be. It can also be useful to discuss this information with a partner to help clarify the role.

If the children are working in one large group the teacher could also join in, in role, as chairperson to enable the smooth running of the proceedings. It is important in this situation to ensure that children do not simply represent stereotypes in role and if this arises to draw attention to it, out of role, to avoid losing the serious nature of the task to a superficial discussion.

It is difficult to suggest how long a meeting in role like this could last. The children often need a little while to get used to the situation, their roles and their arguments, but once the talk becomes repetitive it is time to stop the role play and discuss what the children thought of the information being shared. It may be appropriate at the end to take a vote on what the community would wish to have, but this is not necessary. It may be of more value to continue to look for what is actually happening in the area and what the local community may think.

From this work it is hoped that children develop a clearer understanding of the issues involved in recycling: this includes the processes involved, how natural resources can be used more economically and the part each individual in society can play. It is also important that children have a clear idea of what is available in their own area and how they themselves can support even minor initiatives.

[*Green Teacher* 10]

Supercan

Just when you thought you'd got can recycling all sorted out, here's something *else* to do with them, from Christian Aid education staff.

Make a Supercan

It is suggested that the children work in groups of two to four to make a puppet. The effort put into this is well worth it!

You will need:

2 large catering-size tins (from school kitchens or other catering establishment).
8 middle-sized tins for limbs.
5 small tins for elbows, knees and neck.
2 ham tins for feet.
2 small shallow tins for hands.
2 plastic quiche trays for head.
Glue, scissors, nail, hammer, thin card, material, block of wood, black thread (strong), strong string.
2 lengths of dowelling (40cm each).
Plastic coated garden twist or other, covered thin wire.

Instructions

Make sure all tins are clean and have no sharp edges.

1. Make holes in the tins as shown in Figure 7. Make sure tins are correct way up.

2. Cover all the tins with material using glue. Make holes through the material with nail. If material is slightly wider than tin it can be folded over open end and glued.

3. Put wire loops through holes in tins for knees and at end of arms.

4. *Lower body*. Join the tins together starting from lower body working down the legs to the feet.

5. *Upper body*. Join hands to lower tin of arm. Join rest of arm together and then attach tightly to upper body.

6. *Head*. Put a knot on the end of a piece of strong string. (This

will carry the entire weight of the puppet.) Thread this through the centre hole in large can (upper body) and through the small can for neck. Glue two plastic quiche trays together with string going through the centre. When this is left to dry make sure the end of the string is tied on to the centre of dowelling A. The two pieces of string X, Y stop the head swinging round.

7. Join the two halves of the body at the waist.

8. Add any extra decorations e.g. pockets, shoe laces, collar etc.

9. *To make face.* Cut out oval of card for face slightly larger than circular head. Face can be painted on card or cut out of felt and stuck on card. Use scraps of coloured felt for eyes, lips, nose. Cover rest of head with paper or material. Glue layers of hair on this or use an old wig.

10. Lay the puppet flat on the ground, legs straight, arms lying by side of body. Have string through neck and head fully extended, with dowelling laying at right angles to puppet. Attach black thread to loops at end of arms. Lay out enough thread, to tie the other ends to each end of dowelling A. Put dowelling B on top of A. Attach black thread to loops at knees. Lay out enough thread, to tie the other ends to each end of dowelling B.

Walking your puppet

The full-size puppet is heavy and stands about 1 metre high. It is best operated by two children.

Practice walking. Hold dowelling B horizontally slightly in front of puppet. Lift each end of dowelling vertically to lift knees. Move forward to walk. To move arms lift ends of dowelling A vertically.

Make a family of supercans. Vary the sizes of the cans to make different puppets.

- Use your puppets in a play.
- Try doing the Can Can!
- Read the book *The Iron Man* by Ted Hughes.

[*Green Teacher* 7]

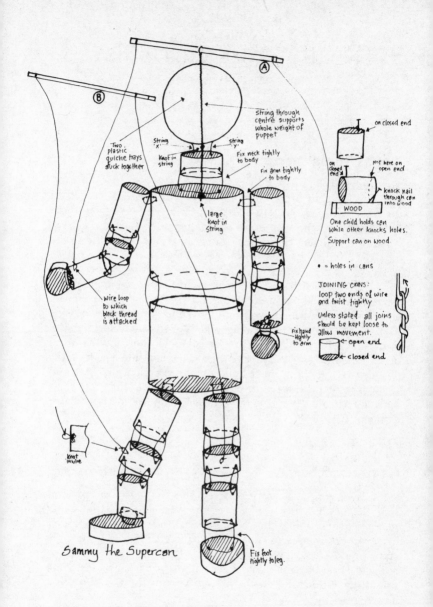

Figure 7: 'Sammy the Supercan'.

9: Really cross curricular

Art as social action

'Art and Development Education, 5–16' was an ILEA curriculum development project run by Aileen McKenzie. It explored the links between these two areas, and in particular how these links enable teachers to tackle issues of gender, race and class.

After this project (Figure 8), it never again makes sense to say 'art is art and those issues belong elsewhere'.

The chart may help you to decide how to assess how engaged your child's education is: *do* social, political and economic issues relate to the production of works of art? The hidden agenda of an art education which avoids all local and global issues outside itself is a reactionary political agenda. Our society has a long way to go along the road of anti-racist education and multicultural development. Art education, which by definition engages the affective in the child, must build on the experience of 'Art and Development Education' in enabling children to integrate their personal artistic development with their empowerment as active democrats.

Green maths?

What messages do we give children and students if we pretend that the maths work we give them is value-free? How many maths teachers think about the political indoctrination implicit in work that refuses to provide or explore data that makes the status quo look dodgy?

Brian Hudson, who now teaches maths teachers, makes some useful suggestions that arose out of a year at the World Studies Teacher Training Centre at York.

My starting point in considering the above question is a view of mathematics as a human activity — in fact an essential aspect of

176

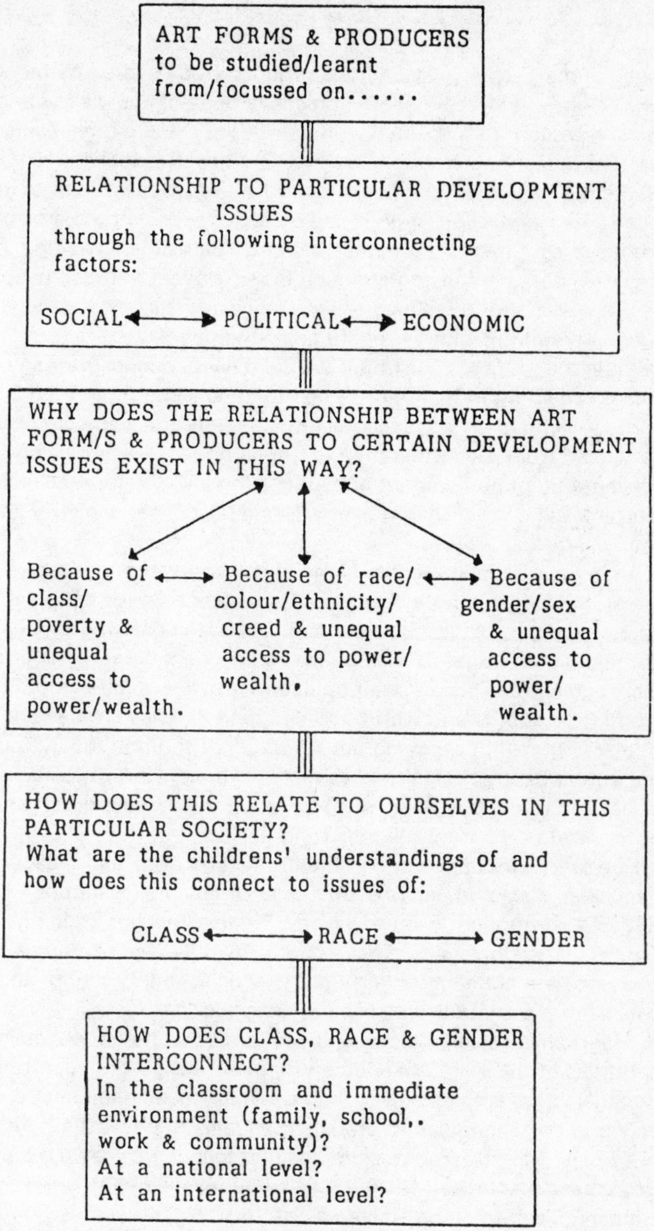

ART FORMS & PRODUCERS
to be studied/learnt
from/focussed on......

RELATIONSHIP TO PARTICULAR DEVELOPMENT
ISSUES
through the following interconnecting
factors:

SOCIAL ←——→ POLITICAL ←——→ ECONOMIC

WHY DOES THE RELATIONSHIP BETWEEN ART
FORM/S & PRODUCERS TO CERTAIN DEVELOPMENT
ISSUES EXIST IN THIS WAY?

Because of ←——→ Because of race/ ←——→ Because of
class/   colour/ethnicity/   gender/sex
poverty &   creed & unequal   & unequal
unequal   access to power/   access to
access to   wealth.   power/
power/wealth.   wealth.

HOW DOES THIS RELATE TO OURSELVES IN THIS
PARTICULAR SOCIETY?
What are the childrens' understandings of and
how does this connect to issues of:

CLASS ←——→ RACE ←——→ GENDER

HOW DOES CLASS, RACE & GENDER
INTERCONNECT?
In the classroom and immediate
environment (family, school,.
work & community)?
At a national level?
At an international level?

Figure 8: 'Art and Development Education, 5–16'. From Green
Teacher *1.*

much human activity. Such a view would not be shared by those who regard mathematics as an objective body of knowledge and skills, divorced from the real world and dominated by mechanistic ways of thinking. Many people have very negative feelings towards mathematics, which are often the result of the presentation of the subject as a collection of pure and objective skills to be mastered. For a subject that is regarded as being concerned solely with the cognitive domain, the contradiction is self-evident in those people who express strong feelings of fear, panic and alienation at any encounter with what they regard as mathematics.

While the process of learning will be a central concern of any teacher claiming to be 'green', I intend to concentrate in this particular article on ways in which mathematical activity can be generated from a consideration of 'green issues'. As such I am concentrating upon content but suggesting also an approach to teaching the subject that implies a less-didactic, participatory and child-centred approach.

An initial task is to identify some of the issues that are central to 'green thinking' — those that stem from a concern for the planet, an awareness of its fragile state and also of the growing threats that loom ever larger. Such issues will include pollution, the arms race, depletion of resources, population growth, famine, and the world food supply and world trade in general. These issues are primarily global but they do nevertheless touch upon the lives of our young people, concerned as many of them are by the nuclear threat and moved by images of starvation in famine-stricken areas of the world on a tragically recurring basis.

However, very little work on the production of suitable resources has taken place and, as a result, this became a major aim of a project that I undertook at the World Studies Teacher Training Centre at the University of York during 1984/85. The resources produced are aimed at older pupils in the secondary school and consist of a computer data base of statistics relating to demographic, social, military and economic factors on 127 major countries of the world. In addition there are supporting classroom materials of examples and problems, which focus upon such issues as world trade, population growth, inequality, the North–South divide etc. The classroom examples that follow are drawn mainly from these resources, which are to be published by the Centre for Global Education at the University of York.

The data base contains twenty fields or items of information on each country listed. These include the population, level of military expenditure, number of doctors, teachers and military personnel, life expectancy, infant mortality rates, rates of access to safe water and details of major arms suppliers.

The information retrieval program will allow information relating to infant mortality rates and levels of military expenditure, for example, to be extracted for each country. This would then enable the student to check for any correlation between the two factors by means of a scatter diagram, for instance. The example which follows (Example 1) illustrates the selective retrieval of information relating to life expectancy and levels of access to safe water for those countries with a life expectancy over 70. The same exercise can be carried out on those countries with life expectancy rates below 50, providing a striking contrast and a clear illustration of the differences in terms of quality of life.

Example 1

The table below shows some of the countries that have a life expectancy of over 70 years. It also contains data on the percentage of the population who have access to safe drinking water.

Country	Life expectancy	Water
United States	75	99%
Canada	75	99%
Argentina	71	60%
Cuba	73	62%
Jamaica	71	82%
Japan	77	98%
Singapore	72	100%
Australia	74	97%
New Zealand	74	93%
Costa Rica	73	81%

(Source — World Military and Social Expenditure, 1983, R L Sivard)

Carry out the calculations necessary to complete the table below.

Life expectancy	Number of countries	Average % for water
77	2	98.5
76		
75		
74		
73		
72		
71		

Comment on the results in your table.

The data base provides the opportunity for further exploration and investigation on the part of the student in a wide variety of ways. The examples that now follow are provided to give more background information and to increase awareness of the complex issues involved. These are of a conventional nature and would best be utilised as and when the student required such further information.

The following example demonstrates the inequality that exists within one particular country and one effect of this. Such examples could obviously be drawn from other countries in the world.

Example 2

The following table gives information relating to income and infant mortality rates (IMR) for New Delhi, India, during the period 1969–74.

Income (rupees per person per month)	IMR (Infant deaths per 1000 live births)
0 – 20	181
21 – 50	82
51 – 100	45
101 – 200	18
201 – 300	14
301 and over	12

(Source: The State of the World's Children, 1984, UNICEF)

(a) *How many times greater is the risk of infant mortality in the lowest income group compared to that in the highest? Give your answer to the nearest whole number.*
(b) *For a family with a newborn child and an income of 35 rupees per*

person per month, what is the probability of the child surviving beyond the infant stage, i.e. to the age of one year?

Further mathematical activity and a greater awareness of another crucial issue can be generated through a consideration of the rate of population growth, as illustrated in the following example.

Example 3

Two thousand years ago the world population was approximately 250 million. By 1830 it had reached 1000 million or 1 billion. The figures in the table below show the significant stages in population growth since that time.

Year	Total World Population (Billions)
1830	1
1925	2
1962	3
1975	4
1985	4.5

(Source: Seeing Green, *Jonathon Porritt)*

(a) *Show these figures clearly on a graph using suitable axis.*
(b) *Use your graph to work out the expected world population in the year 2000.*
(c) *When was the world population half of that given in your answer to part b)?*
(d) *Using your previous answer, work out how long it will have taken for the world population to double itself up to the year 2000.*

Many of these examples give rise to further questions and may prove to be starting points for students to carry out their own research and investigation. One outcome of working in this way will be to reduce the control of the teacher over the content and direction of the lesson. However, this will allow the teacher to develop the role of a facilitator in guiding students along their own chosen paths of enquiry.

There will be times when such an approach to teaching mathematics will be restricted not only by teachers but by students themselves. This will be particularly true of older pupils who have become conditioned into accepting the compartmentalised view of the curriculum with mathematics assigned to a slot completely separate from any other subject. However such a view of mathematics is undoubtedly changing and hopefully any disappointments will soon be outnumbered by the successes. Perhaps the most encouraging response during classroom trials of the WSTTC Project materials came from a member of a fourth year class in an inner-city, multi-racial comprehensive school. His comment also probably provides a fitting judgement on our current educational system and certainly his own experience of it: 'I found the disk (data base) easy to work with, enjoyable and interesting. It tells you things you thought you would never know.'

[*Green Teacher* 1]

10: Schools doing it!

School conservation policy

Steve Byers' school won a 'European Year of the Environment award in 1988, and his work has greatly impressed colleagues at more than one gathering I have been at. Could it give ideas and confidence to a school near you?

Since September 1983, when I was appointed co-ordinator for conservation education at Myers Grove Comprehensive School, my main efforts have gone into the development of environmental aspects of the curriculum. I have recently been putting the final touches to an analysis of the whole curriculum at the school. The aim of this is to find out where, or if, 250 key environmental ideas and issues are taught. This is a much more detailed survey than one I carried out a few years ago. I feel that highlighting the key environmental ideas and issues is essential if the students at the school are to gain a complete environmental education. It will also make much easier the discussions we plan to have with a number of contributory junior schools, the first of which will take place in February on one of the curriculum days.

The general agreement among a number of members of staff on what are the important environmental issues led quite naturally last year to the development of a new environmental foundation course for all first year students. The development of this course has been undertaken in the main by the head of geography and myself. The complete co-ordination of this course with other first year subjects will be our next step.

The co-ordination of environmental themes has also taken place within the third year. Here I have produced a modular biology course, which now includes quite a number of environmental issues that were found to be missing or covered incompletely in my earlier analysis of the curriculum. It has led to the joint teaching of one particular third year environment topic — soil — where biology and geography lessons now complement each other.

The introduction of the GCSE modular Science has provided a good opportunity to improve the environmental education of our students. This course has four core modules, one of which is called 'environments'. Also, three of its option modules concentrate on particularly important resource issues: water, food, waste and pollution. I have been developing and teaching the core modules of GCSE science this year and will begin the teaching of the waste and pollution module soon. I hope to have a major involvement in the development of these environmentally based modules so that when science is introduced for all fourth year students in 1989 they will play a vital role in the composition of the course.

Recently a number of Sheffield teachers, including myself, have been discussing the development and introduction of a new GCSE Mode 3 course called Environment (Issues and Analysis). David Parker of Westfield School has worked hard to get this syllabus approved by the Schools Examination Council. It is a very flexible modular course for the whole ability range. Hopefully it will be possible to introduce this course into Myers Grove in September 1989. Because of its great flexibility (its course contents are designed by the school) it should provide an excellent opportunity to broaden fourth and fifth year students' environmental education without conflicting with what is studied in other subjects.

The school has a very active conservation group, which has undertaken practical projects of direct benefit to the environment. Some of the work that took place last term included: a visit to Edale in Derbyshire to help the National Trust with the repairs they are carrying out to the very eroded paths on Mam Tor; a weekend at Hardwick Hall helping the National Trust tend young oak trees planted to replace old and dying trees; and a weekend in the Lake District helping the National Trust with a number of tasks, e.g. drystone walling.

In November, a very large group of pupils visited our wildlife site on Broadhead Flats Farm in the Loxley valley. Myers Grove School took over the management of this site in 1984 (it had been the site of an old rubbish tip). Our aim was to transform it into a prime wildlife site. Over the past four years hundreds of trees and shrubs have been planted; the banks of a very large pond, excavated on the site, have been turfed; an observation platform at the pond side has been constructed; a network of paths has been started and much more. The original project is far from finished but every year our original objective comes nearer to achievement. Since 1984 well over three hundred different students have worked on the site.

Just before Christmas a group of the school's conservationists visited Monteney Nursery School to repair a small garden that had been vandalised a few weeks earlier. The area was tidied up and replanted with trees and shrubs.

Each April Sheffield holds its Environment Week. This celebration has taken place every Spring since 1985. As a member of the organising committee since its inception in 1984 I have been responsible for co-ordinating schools' involvement in Environment Week. This has entailed producing publicity materials and a complete programme of the week's events in the City's schools. During this week a wide range of schools from nursery and infants to secondary make a special attempt to celebrate their environment by bringing their environmental work to the fore. The production of the schools programme has been sponsored since 1985 by Bassetts Foods PLC. Co-ordinated brilliantly by Roger Butterfield, Environment Week 1987 turned out to be just about the biggest nationally, and certainly anywhere in the North. Sheffield should be pleased with its leading role. The City is beginning to get a green centre and we teachers can help the greening.

[*Green Teacher* 8]

Teach it? Do it!

'Practise what you preach' can be a little unfair if taken to extremes, but there must be many schools teaching about energy and resource saving but doing little about it. Rosemary Jones offers some ideas:

Acting realistically to secure a sustainable future for our children requires more than lip service to the practicalities of resource saving in our educational establishments. But habits die hard and though we know about the damaging effects of over-consumerism on our environment, we still accept wastefulness of materials and inadequate building insulation as normal practice, hardly realising that as an example it is part of the informal educational curriculum, which influences our children's attitudes probably as much as what we officially teach them.

It is certainly surprising, given the cost-effectiveness of energy conservation measures, that so few of our educational buildings have been made energy-efficient. One school that has is Hither Green Primary School in South East London, which was built in

the 1880s and was typical of the thermally heavyweight schools of
that period. Now fuel savings of around 50 per cent have resulted
from roof insulation, boiler sequencing controls and
draughtproofing of windows and entrances. The payback period
on such transforming is usually between two and seven years. In
real terms and in the face of most governments' inability to make
the necessary protective legislation to halt increasing
environmental acidity, the need for such saving is imperative.

Campaigning is always hard work, but if enough teachers and
administrators in an establishment agree to an environmentally
appropriate policy, then a programme for change can be put to the
policy-makers, and, if implemented throughout the education
authority, be made easier and more cost-effective through bulk
buying and co-operative organisation. The following points could
act as a guideline for such a policy.

Energy Monitoring

Savings of 5 per cent upwards on fuel bills are possible from this
action alone, which is best taken over short periods; requires
appointed staff or students to read the meters regularly at the same
time as campaigning for reduced fuel consumption, shutting doors
and windows in winter and limiting heating and lighting needs.

Building Insulation

Draught insulation, double glazing and cavity wall and roof
insulation can reduce fuel bills by 40 per cent.

Appropriate Technology Installation

Thermostat controls, sound-sensitive light and heat controls and
central climatic monitoring, as well as the use of low cost lighting
can give further savings. Information may be obtained from The
Energy Efficiency Office, Milbank, London W1.

Recycled paper use

Increased use of recycled paper could reduce pulp/paper imported
by £400 million annually. As it is, few schools and colleges use
more than a small component in their exercise books and files. Re-
use of envelopes and bulk-buying of recycled paper could reduce

both financial and energy costs. Paperback (01–980 2233) provide the paper.

Recycled paper collection

Prices paid for collected paper vary with its quality and the demand for it, but as one third of our domestic and commercial garbage is paper, dumped in landfill sites when it could be better used as recycled paper, it is worth recycling it for no financial gain at all. Enquiries for collection in your area from LWRA, 01 633 2786.

Can collection

Every thrown can is a loss of about 10p to the consumer. More important it means that basic materials like aluminium and tin are mined from often eco-sensitive areas like the tropical rainforest lands to replace what is dumped on our own environment. Save-A-Can give £8 per tonne to a children's charity for cans returned to them. Can collection, with this added incentive, could be appropriate in primary and secondary schools. Save-A-Can are at Elmhouse, 36 Grosvenor Gdns, London SW1.

Bottle collection

Energy savings on systems that recycle glass cullet are only 5 per cent efficient compared with re-use, which is 25 per cent effective. Demands for returnable bottles in schools and colleges could emphasise the need for such a saving. Local Councils should be asked to implement re-use schemes at the collection depots. Re-use bottles in supermarkets should be chosen.

Healthy food

Healthy food means a healthy countryside as well as health for the people who eat it. It also means fewer demands on the NHS and the drug companies. Food awareness must be every teacher's and parent's responsibility. The Soil Association, 86–88 Colston Street, Bristol, BS1 5BB, will advise on all aspects.

Greening the school or college grounds

Without acclimatisation to plant and animal life in the early school years, it is not sensible to expect appropriate environmental behaviour from urban people in adult life. Transforming exercise yards into gardens may go some way to increase natural awareness. The British Trust for Conservation Volunteers, Wallingford, Oxon, will give advice and some practical help with greening schemes throughout the UK.

Compost making

Worldwide we are losing three tonnes of soil on average per acre, usually because of bad farming practices that refute the Law of Return by not putting back into the soil what is taken out of it. Throwing away surplus foods and sewage is part of this process and if possible such refuse should be kept on viable land rather than dumped at sea or in landfill. Transport costs could be avoided by such measures and the resulting rich soils made use of. Again, local councils should be approached for compost collection.

[*Green Teacher* 10]

Sweet syllabus

Carol Weitz here relates how something dear to the children's hearts provided some unexpected lessons.

Unexpected lesson . . . a sweet idea!

Stretching the theme during a cross-curricular Geography Week, twelve-year-old ESL students set out to find out more about their favourite sweets.

In pockets and schoolbags they soon found wrappers from the last break and were made aware of the small print, lists of ingredients, among them mysterious 'Es' and numbers.

Explaining the purpose of these code numbers for colouring and preservatives, I triumphantly produced a list of them currently being circulated, which claimed the authorship of a French hospital research centre. My copy had been given to a friend by her paediatrician. The list reported the dangerous side-effects of many commonly used food additives.

Grade 6 were vociferous with indignation. A very earnest child, an asthma sufferer, was especially concerned. Good questions were raised, such as, 'How much do you have to eat for it to harm you?' Here and there the 'very last' red and orange fruitgums were chewed. There was a defiant, 'I don't care. They still taste good.'

Homework that day was research at the sweet counter. Meanwhile I was granted £10 to fund my project. with this I bought an alternative selection of sweets, containing none of the suspicious substances.

The children couldn't believe their luck when the next lesson turned out to be a 'candy tasting'. This was executed in a 'scientific manner'. Without passing comments, each student tested the products for colour, smell, consistency and flavour. Notes were taken and then compared.

A new range of 'Tropical Fruits' with natural colouring and flavouring, in an attractive packet, went down very well. One more of a new favourite was proffered, then the rest were safely stored. For the next step, the ideas of 'boycott' and 'propaganda' were introduced. Posters with slogans and with original wrappers glued on were prepared. We were preparing for a 'Safer Candy Sale', to reinforce and pass on what had been learned. We hoped to influence the Student Council tuck shop policy, too.

But another lesson was still to come. I had already received enquiries about this activity from one girl's father who works for a multinational producer of sweets, chocolate and cocoa. Through this channel came the trump in defence of the 'Es'. It was a press release from the Federal German Health Ministry, dated July 21st 1986. It stated that the Villejuifer Hospital Research Centre denied responsibility for the list, 'which was ten years old'. The Ministry's finding was that the latest research did not support it, that substances are subjected to rigorous tests and are only passed when there is no doubt whatsoever about them being safe for health.

Slightly embarrassed I speedily procured information from a third source, the Consumer Advice Bureau. Their latest list of additives was published in February 1987. I was invited to see test reports and case histories in their archives. On comparing the two lists I was able to satisfy myself that it was very largely the same substances that were under fire.

The Consumer Advice report, though more reserved in its judgement, registered detrimental effects in the case of over twenty additives. These include skin allergies, asthma, headaches, nausea, stomach-ache, hyper-activity and concentration problems after normal consumption. In animals used, alas, for tests, various 'Es' were found to cause enlarged livers, epilepsy, intestinal tumours, and stomach cancer.

A large display was set up, showing the three sources of information, the French list dutifully crossed out and labelled 'unauthentic'.

The additional lesson was something like this: 'Don't just believe anything anybody tells you, whether it's your doctor, your teacher or a government ministry!'

The 'Safer Candy Sale' earned a small donation to our Foster Children Fund. One student had tracked down the red E123 banned in the USA since 1976. Three mothers corroborated the findings about hyperactivity after jellies and ice-lollipops.

Yesterday, a couple of months later, I saw some of my class at break, eating green apple-scented 'shoe laces' and lurid blue wine gum smurfs.

[*Green Teacher* 7]

Environmental work in the curriculum

In 1986–87 Mike Parry, a Wolverhampton teacher, studied as a Schoolteacher Fellow at the University of Warwick. His report, which covered thirty-nine schools, from infant to comprehensive, in nine LEAs, is an excellent recent source on why, and how, schools bring environmental education into their curriculum. These extracts should be useful background for insiders and outsiders hoping to see changes in *their* schools. I highly recommend this report.

· **The most important** reason [for introducing environmental education] originating within the school was the headteacher's belief in that which is 'good' education. This was often a general notion arising from intuition and experience. When explained, it included such factors as a desire to concentrate on skills, concepts, attitudes and values and not only on content; a belief in subject integration; a wish to provide more first-hand sensory experiences and a more structured approach to learning. The headteachers' personal interests in outdoor activities and pursuits and their academic backgrounds and curriculum strengths were also of significance.

Conclusion

The management of environmental curriculum innovation needs to start with a recognition of the school's structures and personnel, and their state of development and attitudes. Radical or moderate reforms may be desired, but they can only be instituted, in reality, by the teachers in the classrooms. Philosophies and ideological stances can be explored in terms of both education and environmental awareness, but if we are to tread more lightly on the Earth these must be translated into school practice. Schools are part of a social system and as such are influenced by societal trends. Many schools, however, seem to work in isolation from the wider context of environmental groups and those who have a role in developing good educational work in the schools. Greater co-operation and understanding between all concerned with developing environmental education is part of the management process required in schools and local authorities.

[Parry M., NAEE Occasional Paper no. 11, 1987 — see Chapter 8.]

11: Greening higher education

Top-down teaching revolution

Polytechnics can be conservative places, in teaching methods among other things. Alan Jenkins and David Pepper, at Oxford Poly, tried an experiment. . . .

We expect that most teachers who read *Green Teacher* use methods where the emphasis is on student activity and involvement. This may be because they consider teacher-centred methods, e.g. lectures, hierarchical and authoritarian and incompatible with their green philosophy.

However, we suspect that most green teachers teach, like us, in institutions where the dominant teaching methods are teacher-centred. Certainly in higher education the lecture or teacher-led seminar (which often effectively degenerates into a teacher lecturing) is the norm, despite research evidence and practical experience of its many limitations.

Yet there are also many of our colleagues at Oxford Polytechnic who, as well as ourselves, have developed teaching methods which encourage students to take responsibility for their own learning and that of their fellow students. About 18 months ago we asked ourselves how it would be possible to widen this approach, so that it became more characteristic of the whole institution. Perhaps our experiences could guide readers who want to try something similar in their own school or college.

We came up with a resolution for the Academic Board (the central decision-making body) to designate one week of the spring term as a 'Non-Traditional Teaching Week'. Our resolution said that during this week staff would be:

Encouraged to use teaching methods where the emphasis is on student activity and involvement.
The week will be regarded as a 'no lecturing' week. In it staff will

be advised that they should not lecture. Rather they must cover their
material by using other teaching methods.

Somewhat to our surprise the resolution was passed with little or
no overt opposition. When we devised the idea we did not expect
it to be passed. We expected it to be roundly rejected in arguments
about academic freedom and the value of lectures, and so forth.
Still, we hoped at least to stir up an argument about the
appropriateness of various teaching methods. We did work hard
at getting the resolution passed. Before the debate we sent a draft
to those in 'key positions' (including the Student Union) who we
thought might favour it. We also sent it to key individuals who we
thought might oppose it and tried to engage them in discussion
before it went into the committee structure, before arriving at
Academic Board. In particular we got considerable support from
many staff throughout the institution who agreed with its aim of
widening the use of 'alternative' teaching methods beyond the
converted. We were very fortunate in having a Directorate that
welcomed the proposal and helped to steer it through the key
committees. It was, however, after this had happened, and the
Academic Board's motion had been passed to Faculties and
Departments for 'action', that reactions became a little more mixed.

There were outcries from many staff. In departmental meetings
there were protests about academic freedom, assertions as to the
value of lectures and that they didn't want somebody 'up there'
telling them how to teach. Student reactions varied, partly
depending upon which staff told them about the event. But in a
way such opposition was too late — it had already been decided
that the week was to take place. Before the week, the Polytechnic's
Educational Methods Unit circulated staff with suggestions as to
how to use their teaching time more effectively than by just
lecturing. Various subject groups discussed what initiatives they
could take.

We cannot be certain that all of the Polytechnic's 450 'lecturers'
really abandoned lecturing in favour of less sterile methods. We
did hear that one or two staff did interpret 'no lecturing' to mean
no classes at all. However, the overall impression we got from the
various feedback exercises was that considerable experimentation
took place and that there was much enjoyment.

- **The Law Unit** ran simulation exercises, a video-centred
  discussion and inter-student quiz, while Accounting students

took complete responsibility for the delivery of a lecture and the management of a practical session.

- **Modern Languages** ran a Chinese whispers exercise for students in which they interpreted a selected passage backwards and forwards — French into English — several times before comparing the final version with the original. Other students enjoyed a game of Trivial Pursuits in Spanish.

- **Education students** spent one day in school, acting as consultants to teachers and undertaking administrative tasks for the school. Another group took responsibility for a Display Workshop, deciding in advance on the content, format and timing of the session. One Education lecturer invited students to write a self-assessment in their Record Books of School Experience, a task usually done by the lecturer, and then compared these with her unofficial notes on their work.

- **Students of Architecture** were asked as an exercise in drawing up typologies to classify an 18th century Irish song as depicted in recordings from round the world. Another class took the opportunity to start a three-week simulation game which debated the redesign, proposed by students, of the St Clements area of Oxford.

- **Two Mathematics lecturers** chose to present a lecture on Hypothesis Testing as a team with scripted dialogue and stage directions in which they challenged each other at agreed (and some disagreed) points. In another class students taught their solutions to problems to other groups. Mathematics were also taught through computer-based simulations.

- **One Psychology lecturer** neatly wove the basic concepts of psychoanalysis into the format of a well-known song which she invited the students to sing!

- **In Geography** students received one lecturer's notes, interspersed with questions, a week in advance so that the greater part of the lecture period could be given over to questions and discussion. Another lecturer asked his class to research in pairs aspects of the geography of China after Mao, and (congruently) to report their findings in a poster. Finally each pair designed an exam question based on the material. Perhaps the most creative event in Geography was the series of short plays performed by two lecturers. The dramatic scenes depicted some of the familiar problems for project students let loose on

the community — unpreparedness, lateness, interviewing a
harrassed, hurried passer-by on a rainswept street, and being
trapped by the local 'Ancient Mariner'!

- **Town Planning** students spent the whole week showing video
  films, which they had made on location over the previous two
  weeks, of a historical or theoretical topic in the context of Oxford.
  In another exercise students role played various national and local
  agencies in a 3-hour simulated debate on an inner city problem.

As a complete antidote to all the heady excitement of the week
the Students' Union held a 'Most Boring Lecture' competition which
was won with consummate ease by the Academic Secretary, who
was adjudged guilty of repetition, delay, talking to the blackboard,
using statistics without explanation, being unprepared, and
encouraging no student involvement. The Students' Union was
kind enough to express the sincere hope that he would remain as
administrator.

It was very good to learn just how widespread was the use of
'alternative methods' throughout much of the institution (and often
in areas such as accountancy which our 'liberal' prejudices might
not have considered) and of the ingenuity of staff and students in
devising and using alternatives to the traditional lecture. There were
some vigorous and often heated discussions in the coffee room
and in the bar. Staff argued about the appropriateness of alternative
teaching methods and of such a week. As we had hoped, designating
a specific week in which all staff and students were to participate
forced attention on the issues we had hoped to raise. As for the
long-term impact of the week, and whether it stimulated more staff
to make changes in their approach to teaching, we are not sure.
Though we have evidence that some staff (including ouselves) have
continued with some of the methods we tried out that week, no
full-scale evaluation was carried out. We do know that other
institutions, like Bristol Polytechnic, have adopted the idea. This
year at Oxford Polytechnic there is to be a somewhat similar event,
but it will be voluntary. Perhaps that is more appropriate. It is less
hierarchical and authoritarian. But will it be so successful in taking
the message to the unconverted? Do you think that any of these
ideas could be relevant to your institution?

[*Green Teacher* 8]

The Green College

Higher education in Britain will never be the same again (we hope!)

The Green College is a new, independent, international residential college which seeks to promote ecocentric values through teaching, research and networking. It is a non-profitmaking institution. The college also works for changes aimed at creating a more sustainable, democratic and egalitarian society. The college runs general interest courses, training courses, credit-earning courses for students on undergraduate degree courses, and distance-learning courses.

The Green College began its activities in January 1989 with a number of public meetings and seminars in London on environmental topics. We ran a successful Summer School in August which attracted participants from Britain, America and several European countries. Our programme for the rest of the year includes:

- a number of weekend courses on topics like Green Parties in Europe, The Agricultural Crisis and Alternative Farming Methods, and The New Economics.
- a series of weekly talks on green issues to be held at St James's Church, Piccadilly, London over a six months period starting in September 1989.
- a sixth form conference in London in October on Environmental Politics. This will be the first of a series of sixth form conferences on green issues.
- In addition, we are also doing some publications on green issues.

In spite of these rather diverse activities, it should be stressed that our primary objective is the establishment of a residential college which will offer a full range of credit-earning courses covering a wide range of green topics. These courses will begin in January 1990.

The Green College runs both full-time and part-time courses. Some are highly specialised and will appeal to people already sympathetic to green thinking. Others are aimed at a wider public. The college caters for the following kinds of students:

- Full-time and part-time students pursuing credit-earning courses for a term or a year. To begin with most of these students will be American and European.

- Students from British schools, further and higher education institutions attending day or weekend courses.
- Students pursuing distance-learning courses.
- Students on residential courses of varying duration, aimed especially at members of the Green Movement, both in Britain and abroad.
- Training courses for environmental groups, private companies and government agencies both in Britain and abroad.
- Courses aimed at the general public.
- Travel-based courses which will enable students to visit innovative projects of interest to environmentalists in Britain and various European countries.

The Green College is a learning community. It aims for excellence in its teaching and, unlike most British institutions of higher education, it gives serious and critical attention to questions of pedagogy. Much of the teaching is based on seminar work in small groups, but there is also a strong emphasis on experiential learning and independent study. In addition, The Green College runs an internship programme which ensures that full-time students can complement their academic studies by gaining practical work experience in the worlds of business, commerce and finance, government agencies, education, the media and voluntary organisations, including environmental groups. The Green College also strives to ensure that its organisational structures and teaching processes are congruent with the values that it seeks to promote.

Further details — see Resources.

New University

It seems a long time since Stephen Hancock wrote this introduction to the latest flowering of green idealism in education: an alternative university in Birmingham. It has since run dozens of courses at the Hockley house, large-scale gatherings in rural Herefordshire, and gone from strength to strength.

Towards a new university

Criticisms of our limited and limiting further education system abound. And, more often than not the criticisers and their criticisms become quieter and quieter, increasingly daunted by the overwhelming and institutional momentum of our polytechnics, universities, colleges and their educational 'outlook': the unquestioned perpetuation of destructive value systems, the narrow-minded specialisation, the careerist orientation, the divisive competition. So why not try to imagine an alternative: of educational networks rather than funnels; of centres which act as a catalyst for people's enthusiasm, pooled resources, shared skills and knowledge; where learning how to repair your bike or insulate your home is as much a part of the educational process as studying the Enlightenment, and is recognised as such, where such courses as co-operative management don't just prepare you for some cut-throat business world *out there*, but help you learn how to create more the sort of living and working environment and structures that you would like to see.

The New University Project is one attempt to realise such visions. The ideas are not particularly new, and the Project's size, at present, seems fairly insignificant. However, if we build our new structures in the shadows of the old carefully enough, with undaunted persistence we might well find ourselves in the ruins of the old, offering much-needed accommodation. The Project has been in the air for about three years and it is this winter that it is to become manifest: the New Educational Housing Co-operative (Ltd) has purchased a house in Hockley, Birmingham, around which the Project will be consolidated, co-ordinated and expanded. At present, 200 or so people have sent back 'feedback forms', giving an outline of their involvement with the Project — ranging from moral support to full-time residence, the skills and knowledge they are prepared to share, and the areas that they seek to learn more about. Interests range from carpentry to humanistic psychology, alternative technology to street theatre. Many people are prepared to come and initiate courses and workshops on weekend, week-long or weekly bases. We are constantly discovering people and groups in or around Birmingham who have expressed interest in being involved with the Project and sharing resources. An advert in the *New Internationalist* has provoked reactions (interested ones) from Singapore to South Africa.

My involvement and excitement with the Project stems from disillusionment with the educational processes I have been through, coupled with glimpses of how it could be — memories of encouragement, creativity, of how amazingly industrious I can be when motivated by my own enthusiasm, and, especially, those moments when I have been 'allowed' to go off at tangents (relative to the set course) in excited pursuit of some knowledge or activity.

Being part of a system that relies overwhelmingly on external assessment and meeting imposed requirements is not only stifling — it is irresponsible. An essence of education — the ability to respond — is severely limited. Active involvement in really influencing and shaping one's educational environment is rare. Talk of student loans and the increasing investment of big business in further education all add to the careerist pressure upon students, whose vision and efforts become fixed upon that final degree or diploma. Room for self-assessment is virtually nil, and struggle against the patronising and pressurising educational set-up is draining (although there are glimmers of hope). There is precious little questioning of the morality of the process in which students find themselves — hence the majority of our further education 'products' go on to perpetuate unjust economic systems and military momentum, all of which will be (and already is for many) the death of us. The need for a creative alternative is paramount.

A word that is used a lot in The New University Project is holistic or 'wholeistic': combining the practical and the intellectual, seeing and exploring the relationships between the themes and subjects that we encounter, giving attention to living together ('But I'm not down on the washing up rota') as well as to some in-depth revolutionary thesis. Room for looking for non-Western ideas, for studying green economics, African drumming, recycling projects, for deciding one's own fields of learning, and for breaking down the traditional divide between 'teacher' and 'taught'.

There are eight of us moving into the Birmingham house this winter, and we hope to start the purchase of another house soon after. We'll be involved in co-ordinating the Project — answering enquiries, writing articles, providing speakers, helping set up similar ventures and so on.

We'll arrange our own individual studies, study some area together, help initiate courses for people in and around Birmingham, provide a newsletter, ensure the mortgage repayments, set up a wholefood co-op, open up our resources to the local community, entertain visitors, convert the cellar rooms, have nervous breakdowns and extended breakfasts. . . .

Hopefully, many other people will become involved in the running of the Project — the main qualification being enthusiasm rather than money or exam results. Continual self-criticism is vital for the Project if it is to avoid introspection and attract and encourage those people and groups in our society usually excluded from the further education system. The avenues of mutual aid and shared skills and knowledge are relatively unexplored *consciously* in the educational process — the potential of resultant networks is far-reaching. A little more mutual respect, concern, sharing and self-respect can go a long way.

This is just the beginning, and we need all the help we can get. Perhaps the course of the Project will go in unforseen directions. If you have any interest whatever in the New University and if you feel you have anything to offer please get in touch.

[*Green Teacher* 2]

12: Local and *very* local

Playground learning

The Coombes School at Arborfield, Reading, is well known for its ground-breaking approach to the use of the school grounds for learning. Headteacher Susan Humphries explains. . . .

Creating a resource for environmental education 'on the doorstep'

At the Coombes, we have tried over the last fifteen years to create an outdoor environment that is satisfying for us all to work and play in, that pleases the eye, and that offers diversity, interest, colour and imaginative scope.

Good play requires an appropriate setting, which meets children's needs. All the environmental improvements we have undertaken since the school opened in 1971 have been based on this premise. The setting in which the child grows and the adult functions is of vital importance, and will colour the way in which we all view the world, our understanding of it, and our relationship with it.

Starting from a rectangle of bare tarmac, we have, over the years, developed a landscape that is varied, full of colour and life, and constantly changing. Our first task was to break up the expanse of flat tarmac by building walls, changing levels (building up banks, constructing steps etc.), and creating pockets of interest (a walled mini-beast sanctuary, a hexagonal castle, ponds, bog garden, spaces for vegetables, plants and trees etc.)

Children need to have a choice of location in which to play: somewhere to hide, somewhere to run, somewhere to be quiet, somewhere to be taller than anyone else, somewhere to sit in comfort, somewhere to be adventurous, somewhere to retreat and somewhere to be brave.

Monochromatic tones are not children's natural choice: they prefer colour, and the brighter the better. We use copious quantities of whatever paint we can lay our hands on, to paint

201

designs on the playground floor, to add colour to playground equipment, to give walls added interest, and to enhance the whole outdoor area. Combined with our planting programmes, the outdoor area has splashes of colour throughout the seasons.

We believe that it is important to offer children a variety of textures and surfaces in the playground, so we have built brick walls, used breeze blocks and cement to erect a variety of structures (castle, look-out tower, nature trail), set wooden tables and benches around the grounds, brought in large logs for the children to climb on, built free-standing structures (saddle, stepping stones, hollow concrete blocks, tunnel, large tyres), obtained boats to be played in, and regularly place carpets for the children to lie on. We offer the children a variety of playground equipment and surfaces, at different heights: our philosophy is that we need to give the same degree of thought and care to the outdoor environment, as we do to the indoor school.

Every year, each child plants and harvests a variety of crops — sunflowers, potatoes, marrows, pumpkins, artichokes, peas, beans, rhubarb, tomatoes, spring flowering bulbs and corms, and wild flowers. They also plant indigenous trees to add to our woodland areas, and harvest top fruits (apples, pears, plums, cherries, conkers, acorns, sweet chestnuts, mulberry, medlar, quince) from trees planted by other children over the last few years. The grounds support a number of chickens, and we keep two sheep (one of which has recently lambed) at the school, in order to put the children into present contact with fast-disappearing rural traditions, and to give them a direct experience of the cyclical and continuing nature of life. The children's first explorations into the environmental sciences are catered for, and we also have the scope to introduce them to physics, chemistry and the like, in our outdoor environment. We aim to offer the children a direct involvement with the natural world.

Much of the children's scientific work is catered for within the school grounds, and this also holds true for other curriculum areas. Maths, language, craft, PE, music, drama and the humanities are given additional impetus when we place them in the context of the children's immediate experience and environment. For instance, the maths games painted in the playground are reproduced on a smaller scale on vinyl sheets for use in the maths room: what the child learns on a more formal basis indoors is also a part of their play time in the grounds. Our hope is that the children will use the

grounds to deepen their understanding, and to widen the scope of their intellectual development, through play.

We all learn best and most effectively when we are enjoying ourselves, having fun, and when the constraints upon us are least. Play, both free and structured, provides the means by which we develop an understanding of the world around us, come to grips with abstract concepts or new ideas, and learn to handle these for ourselves: the setting for that play has an implicit importance. The drab uniformity of many school grounds does little to enhance the lives of the children who are confined to them: we need to reflect

on the quality of school landscapes, and to attempt to offer the children in our care the very best that we can.

Every one of us is a product of the environment in which we live and work: at the Coombes, we are trying to provide a setting that will feast the eye, the ear, the nose, the intellect, and the inner heart of all those who use the school.

[*Green Teacher* 4]

Design your playspace. . . .

The Islington Schools Environment Project (ISEP) works with teachers and parents, transforming barren areas at schools into exciting play spaces, with the children doing the design work. The ISEP team take the children through a truly participatory design process, with some amazingly imaginative results, using a specially-developed design kit. The children end up with not only their own, *owned* play equipment, but with training in democratic design, and experience of taking hold of an important area of their lives. The ISEP team have produced 'Playstructures', a report on their work with one school, in conjunction with CSV: details in Resources.

As a result of concerns about design participation by children, a kit has recently been developed that reproduces those elements of playstructure design that we know work — tyres, poles, ropes, chains, platforms and hand-rails — in a miniature form.

We provide a design language that is appropriate for children in terms of their ability to use and manipulate the elements. We limit the components to those known to be appropriate for use in schools. And we turn the information on the objective constraints that limit the range of designs into a form that children can apply to their own work.

> The imaginative use of materials and the range of work that could be construed as sculpture was a terrific stimulus to the pupils.
>
> Once the children were familiar with the contents and possibilities of the kit, each child had the opportunity to make his or her design for the playground to scale.

Two playstructures were built in the playground [of the Winton School] and are now in use. The school community designed them. The idea was to reduce the designer's involvement to the role of the adviser, consultant or trainer, so that the bulk of the work would be carried out by the teachers and children without a designer working directly in the classroom.

The kit was also designed to be used as an aid for learning more formal skills in mathematics and as a stimulus for exploring issues related to play and the playground.

Children greatly enjoyed using the kit and some teachers felt that it would be valuable as an educational toy and tool to be permanently part of the school resources.

One of the advantages of working with a model-making kit in designing playstructures is that it allows people to participate effectively in the important discussions and decision-making that are part of a community design process.

[From *Playstructures* by Patrick Allen]

Using local issues — a plea

Julian Agyeman works in environmental education in Lambeth and is concerned, amongst other things, with who actually *partici-*

Figure 9: (a) Using models to design the playground. (b) The two playstructures in the playground.

Wendnesday March 5th
          My playstructure
My playstructure was made with
lots of logs and tyres. And
it has lots of clips and you
can swing on it. And my
playstructure is not safe and you
can fall off easily. And I could
add a net to it. I could fit
a barrier round it so that is
would stop other children running
into the swings when the other
children are on them.

pates in those local issues in which teachers often assume that 'localness' is sufficient to make their study relevant. In using local environmental data or conflicts, who participates and why they do while others do not can be the hidden, most important, issue.

I want, using a case study, to illustrate two inter-related points (pleas):

1. In using the local environment as a resource, do not let the particular issue under study dominate a wide range of supporting or associated issues.

2. In studying say, an inner-city land-use conflict, we all too often use role-plays of those who participated e.g., planner, local resident, amenity society, developer etc. What about those who did not participate?

A case study: Shakespeare Road Sidings, Brixton

1. The site

- A former railway sidings on the London–Chatham–Dover line, rails removed in 1960.

- Status prior to July 1986: early successional birch woodland with central grassland ride.

- Rare species (for London) included bee orchid, eyebright and musk thistle.

2. Planning history

- BR-owned until November 1984.

- Auctioned to Mr King, property developer, for £115,000.

- April 1985, Mr King submits planning application for 50 two-storey houses. Application deferred from June planning committee.

- November 1985, London Wildlife Trust submit application for an environmental teaching centre and nature park.

- February 1986, LWT application approved, Mr King's deferred.

- June 1986, Mr King's application refused.

- July 1986, Mr King bulldozes site, member of LWT injured by bulldozer.
- July 1986, Council and LWT call local public meeting to decide what to do.
- November 1986, Compulsory Purchase Order on Mr King, appeal by Mr King against refusal.
- July 1987, Public Inquiry to hear CPO and appeal.
- December 1987, decision?

A typical inner-city land-use conflict; environmental pressure group (LWT) and borough council versus developer. On one level, teachers could use this to illustrate the need for semi-natural green space in inner-cities. This, after all, is the 'particular issue' mentioned in point (plea) (i). However, in using solely the 'particular issue', a wealth of supporting or associated issues may be missed.

To investigate these, look at the statistics in Tables 1 to 6, which are socio-economic profiles of people who attended the public meeting after the bulldozing of the sidings, in July 1986.

Table 1 Housing profile

	1	2	3
	%	%	%
Owner-occupier	63.0	35.0	26.6
Housing Association	11.0	19.1	6.7
Private rented	7.5	22.6	23.5
Local Authority	7.5	23.1	43.1
Other	11.0*	0.2	0.1

*Exclusively co-operative dwellers.
Group 1 = participants in public meeting. Group 2 = population of Herne Hill Ward. Group 3 = population of London Borough of Lambeth.

Table 2 Educational profile

	1	4
	%	%
CSE/'O'-Level/'O' Grade	11.0	26.0*
'A'-Level/Highers/B Tech	13.0	15.0
Degree/HND/Higher Degree	62.0	6.0
Student (Full-time)	3.0	5.0
No qualification/response	11.0(n.r.)	48.0(n.q.)

*Includes commercial/apprentice qualifications.
Group 1 = participants in public meeting. Group 4 = national statistics.

Table 3 Employment profile

	1	3	4
(a) Percentages employed			
	%		
Full-time (30 hr/week)	57.0		
Non-full-time (less than 30 hr/week)	32.0		
Retired	8.0		
Student (full-time)	3.0		
(b) Employment type (full-time)			
	%	%	%
Managerial professional (AB)	65.0	13.0	14.0
Technical/clerical (C1)	35.0	37.0	22.0
Skilled/manual (C2)	5.0	23.0	31.0
Unskilled manual (DE)	0.0	27.0	33.0

Group 1 = public meeting. Group 3 = population of London Borough of Lambeth. Group 4 = national statistics.

Table 4 Membership of environmental organisations

	1	4
	%	%
Members	70.0	10.0
Non-members	30.0	90.0

Group 1 = participants in public meeting. Group 4 = national statistics.

Table 5 Ethnic origin

	1	2	3	4
	%	%	%	%
White	95.0	75.0	76.0	95.6
NCWP/black	5.0	24.4*	24.0	4.4

*Up to 40% in some areas.
Group 1 = participants in public meeting. Group 2 = population of Herne Hill Ward. Group 3 = population of London Borough of Lambeth. Group 4 = national statistics.

Table 6 Attendance on part-time further education courses (day or evening)

	1	4
	%	%
Attenders	30.0	4.0
Non-attenders	70.0	96.0*

*Includes 5% full-time students.
Group 1 = participants in public meeting. Group 4 = national statistics.

Housing, education, employment, membership of environmental organisations, ethnic origins and attendance on part-time FE (day or evening) courses, all indicators of socio-economic status, show the nature of participation in this issue. From such statistics, non-participation can be seen to be predominantly working-class and black.

Using a slide show of the case-study and an outline of the planning history, together with the above statistics, I attempted to find some answers from young, predominantly black students at Brixton College and South London College (Knights Hill). They were not surprised by the results. Their analyses, listed below, have implications for all environmentalists.

a. No-one listens to black people, what's the point of venturing an opinion?

b. Getting a job, good education and housing are more important.

c. Pressures from within 'the community' to explore only 'safe' territories e.g., sport, entertainment etc., preclude environmental participation amongst young blacks.

The students were adamant that non-participation was *not* due to lack of interest but lack of time, time in the sense that, until their more pressing needs were fulfilled they would not participate in what they considered to be an extravagance.

After having studied the Shakespeare Road Sidings conflict for two years, and having used the 'particular issue' and associated issues together with 'who did not participate' in classroom simulations, I can guarantee that all students who have been through the exercise found it revealing. As an inner-city environmental educationalist, I see an ever-increasing need for environmental issues such as the Shakespeare Road Sidings conflict to be analysed in the context of social, political economic and cultural factors.

To ignore these issues is wrong. After all, the environment does not create conflict: people, with their political economic and cultural systems, do.

[*Green Teacher* 7]

Inside outside

The 'Tidy Britain Group' publishes some excellent material for schools and teachers, a million miles on from their origins in 'Keep Britain Tidy'. Planning, designing and producing a better school environment is what this 1988 publication (Figure 10) is all about — and very useful it is.

Work with children aimed directly at improving their school environment brings, The Tidy Britain Group's research found, a *very* wide range of curricular benefits.

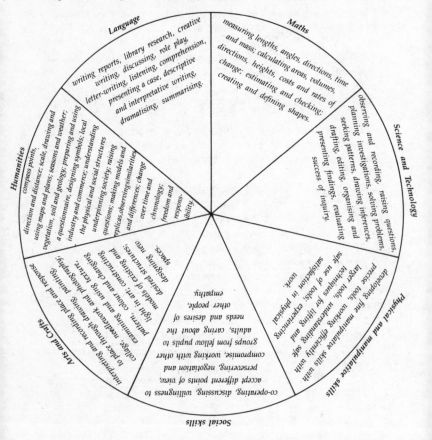

Figure 10: The planning process and the curriculum. From Mares, Cherry and Robert Stephenson, Inside, Outside.

13: Changing schools

The *New Internationalist* whole-person High School seems like a good place. . . .

1. Students

People from 2 to 92. There is no reason why school should be a one-off event for the young. Elderly people and infants are just as capable of learning as children and teenagers. And they are often more willing students: the old bring years of experience to their lessons, the young want to explore the world in their own way. Learning should be a lifelong experience.

2. Facilities

An old grey stone building with chapel and playing fields; a clearing in the forest; a tent; a tin hut. Many poor countries have shown that a good school is simply that place where pupils empower themselves, and the teachers believe in the abilities of their students. Expensive resources may make school life easier. But they are not crucial. Equipment can be improvised and the improvisation is itself a form of learning.

3. Staff

Our teachers enjoy learning as well as teaching. And our best teachers work with learners who have the greatest difficulties. Everyone has to take a turn at administration and course development. Nobody is encouraged through promotion or higher pay to leave teaching for an administrative job.

the **N** whole·person High School

CREDO

All pupils are gifted pupils

I must attend equally to all pupils

All pupils are capable of
concentration and persistence

School is more interesting
than mass entertainment

4. Curriculum

We use the whole brain at our school. We cultivate intuitive, numerical, artistic, mechanical, philosophical, practical, social and logical skills. Nobody is excluded from any subject. Farmers study classical languages, scientists study child-care, musicians motor-mechanics. Our *only* compulsory subjects are the ones you need in order to learn everything else; reading, writing, number, observation, rhetoric and conscientisation (challenging everything).

5. Teaching Methods

Our teachers have to repeat every morning

All pupils are gifted pupils
I must attend equally to all pupils
All pupils are capable of concentration and persistence
School is more interesting than mass entertainment.

With these rules in mind the teachers use play, discovery, rote-learning, repetition, problem-solving or games, depending on the subject, the learner and what works. Our teachers don't follow methods blindly.

6. Examinations

Our graduates never graduate, because we believe that learning should never end. All our tests and exercises have only one purpose: to show teacher and learner their progress towards the goals they have set. Our exams are for information only. Nobody fails exams here, because failure destroys curiosity and confidence. We believe that we just cannot afford failure.

7. Fees

None. What is not provided collectively is produced from our own work. At The New Internationalist Whole Person High School, school and work co-exist at all ages. Nobody is permitted just to study and neglect the routine work of the community. And nobody is expected to work and not have time to study.

[*New Internationalist* 180]

Small School

There are several small schools, but just one with the above name. Theresa West, who works at the school, wrote about it.

The Small School is the secondary school in North Devon from which grew the campaign for schools to be run on 'humanscale' principles. What those principles are, exactly, was a question much worried over at the Oxford conference [of the Human Scale Education Movement: see Chapter 4].

The Schumacher Society both helped found the Small School and sponsored the conference, and the school now serves as an established working model: an essential resource in the campaign. Has any other reform proposal had such a working prototype?

There was a secondary school in Hartland until the 1960s, when the DES decreed that it was no longer viable. Children from Hartland and other local primary schools travel by several coaches to Bideford, an hour away, or are driven by their parents to Bude, 20 miles away in Cornwall. Some, and the number increases every year, come to the Small School.

The schoolhouse is a converted Methodist chapel and two adjoining cottages in the main street of the village. The buildings were bought by Satish Kumar, president of the Schumacher Society, at auction. Shares were sold to private investors, and a trust fund was established; this fund owns the buildings. That was in August 1982. The school opened with nine children and one full-time teacher the following September.

The parents of those first nine children could not go along with the idea of their children being driven 15 miles to and from school, into a community where they were unknown, to attend a school with some 1,800 pupils. They considered their children still young enough to need a more friendly environment; one or two of the children had no experience of school, having been educated at home.

E. F. Schumacher, author of *Small is Beautiful*, introduced ideas on economics which are gradually being accepted by industry. The group responsible for the Small School felt that those ideas might also be applied to education. In September 1983, Colin Hodgetts, a former Director of Christian Aid, warden and chaplain of the Othona Interdenominational Community, and co-ordinator of refugee projects with the Save the Children Fund, was persuaded by Satish Kumar to return to teaching and to join the campaign for Human Scale Education. He was appointed headteacher of the Small School.

The school in Hartland is governed by the Small School Society, to which all children, parents and teachers belong. It is a charitable trust. There are two full-time teachers and, at last count, 16 visiting and part-time teachers, drawn from parents and people working in the neighbourhood. There are 30 pupils, aged from 11 to 16. The school's running costs are met by charitable grants, by teachers and helpers taking small salaries, and by parents. For the first four years, grants were the main source of funding, but charities will generally only meet running costs at the beginning of a new project. When initial funding ceased, it was agreed that parents should be responsible for raising a quarter of the school's annual running expenses, and that a parent would work part-time on obtaining new charitable grants. That quarter was divided amongst the number of children, and a nominal fee of £100 per term was agreed, to be paid by parents who can afford it. Parents unable to pay may perform some service, and at present the services being given include typing, the teaching of typing, weaving, sewing and Italian. Maintenance work, goods, or food may also be given.

Food is as local as possible, from the village, from parents' smallholdings and from the school garden. Meals are vegetarian, not from any wish to advocate vegetarianism, which would be inappropriate in a school where many children come from beef and dairy farming backgrounds, but for reasons of economy and hygiene. Lunch, which includes bread baked daily by the children, is prepared on four days a week by two children and Caroline Walker, housekeeper and cook. On one day a week, lunch is planned, shopped for, cooked and served by three older children. Washing up, clearing tables and sweeping the floor are done by the children and teachers, on a rota. Children who have come from other schools have to reappraise teacher/pupil roles when the headteacher helps them with the washing up. The children also work in groups at the end of the day in hoovering, dusting and tidying up, after which there is a short winding-down session for retrieving personal property, for notices and for discussion.

School days begin with a half-hour assembly, which always includes a song, a story or reading, and a short silence. Teachers take it in turns to lead assembly. There is discussion of world or local affairs, and plans for the day ahead. During the first week of the Michaelmas term, with seven newcomers, GCSE courses, over thirty subjects, and thirty children — each of whom had the chance to organise his/her programme of work afresh — there was much discussion of the day ahead. For Colin, and for Maggie Agg, a science specialist and the school's other full-time teacher, it was a huge task to arrange everyone's timetable to everyone's satisfaction. They did this by amassing a multitude of small rectangles of paper of many colours which, once collated, would solve everything. Each should have had written on it by children, a name and a subject. They didn't always. Some children take pleasure in timewasting. Happily, in a small school the writing is recognisable.

There is a compulsory core curriculum: English, Maths, Humanities, some form of physical recreation, and Science. All children are encouraged to choose a practical subject, from building, gardening, woodwork, weaving, cheese-making, sewing and knitting. All are encouraged to join art, pottery, music and drama groups. Each child negotiates an individual curriculum from what is on offer, and each curriculum must fill a week.

This will be the first year of GCSEs. Last year two pupils joined the school some way through their 'O' level courses and carried on, with good results. One fourteen-year-old gained a grade A in 'O' level Art. Several who are to take GCSEs this year have been somewhat hindered by the courses that never came, or came too late. Courses have been found that may be followed by everyone, but not everyone will have to submit their work to the examining boards for a certificate. The unanimous view of the school's governing Society is that gaining GCSEs should not become priority in a child's education, should not dominate the curriculum (each child may take up to five subjects only), and should not be seen as a whole assessment of a person's five years in a secondary school. Flexibility is possible in a small school, and so the group of four who should have begun their courses last year will follow a one-year course aimed at more mature students. Should any wish, as last year when one 15-year old gained an RSA 2 qualification in typing, it is also possible to work for other qualifications.

The question of the maximum number of children possible in a humanscale school is often raised. The answer has been that when it is no longer possible for all the teachers to know all the children — and all the parents — the school is too big. For the Small School, the size of the buildings limits the maximum at present to 36. With 30 on roll, the school can no longer take children who do not live in the catchment area. There are constant enquiries from all over England and abroad, from parents wanting places for their children, and from teachers and students seeking inspiration. It is to be hoped that the lessons being learned from the Small School, and from the support network of the Campaign for Humanscale Education, will encourage the founding of similar schools. Funding seems in fact to be the only stumbling block: surely there is some EEC irregularity here, when it is national policy in Denmark and in Holland that groups of parents or other organisations are entitled to government funding to run their own schools? As it is, there are emerging several small schools, not all in a 'rural idyll' as the Hartland school has been described (and therefore supposedly inappropriate for inner city areas).

[*Green Teacher* 6]

For a very recent experience of starting a small school, *with* local authority approval and assistance, look at Oaktree, in Liverpool, the brainchild of a wonderful woman, Sister Marie Fillingham (address in 'Resources').

The educational process: towards self-actualisation

Carl Rogers refers to 'Man's tendency to actualise himself, to become his potentialities, the urge to expand, extend, develop, mature, to express and activate all the capacities of the organism to the extent that such activities enhance the self.' Alan Rees, at Garnett College, Thames Polytechnic, teaches students about the 'process model', which is much influenced by Rogers. He offers a useful comparison chart.

Two educational paradigms

1 Emphasis on **content**; on transmission of knowledge/information; or how to **answer** questions; on **destination**.

2 Emphasis on rewarding **conformity/agreement**.

3 Curriculum **imposed** — specified in advance. Detailed, specific **objectives**.

1 Emphasis on **process**: on access to knowledge/information; on 'learning how to learn', how to **ask** questions; on **journey**.

2 Emphasis on rewarding **disagreement/dissent**.

3 Curriculum **negotiated**. Broad general **aims**.

4 Emphasis on **'book'** knowledge and **compartmentalised** subjects.

4 Emphasis on **'common core'** and **integrated** topics.

5 Emphasis on **'skills'/'competencies'**.

5 Emphasis on **'experience–reflection'** learning.

6 Emphasis on **performance**.

6 Emphasis on **self-image** as a factor determining performance.

7 Personal feelings **discouraged**.

7 Personal feelings **explored**.

8 Emphasis on analytical, convergent 'closed' reasoning: 'right' answers.

8 Emphasis on intuitive guesswork: analytical thinking; 'open', divergent thinking; alternative possibilities.

9 Emphasis on comparison, competition, and **external assessment**.

9 Emphasis on achieving potential, on group co-operation, and **self-assessment**.

10 Emphasis on fixed limits, determined by ability — on labelling/low expectation.

10 Emphasis on going beyond perceived limits; on high expectation.

11 Classroom space reflects **transmission**.

11 Classroom space reflects **interaction** and **exchange**.

12 Emphasis on educational technology as aids to learning, e.g. computers.

12 Emphasis on relationships as aids to learning.

Checklist

The questions in the checklist below are offered as the beginning of a process. There are great dangers in that process, even in beginning it, but if we are to take action co-operatively, parents and teachers, we must begin with parents becoming informed in ways which have not happened before now.

Please don't regard these particular questions as tablets of stone: do add to the list, subtract from it, change any or all of them. The list is a beginning, a baseline from which to start. Some questions run into and overlap with others: in some cases this is unfortunate but inevitable, in others it is intentional, to get different angles on the same topic. It is, too, rather a long list, again intentionally so. You won't want to use them all at once: just select what you feel the school can cope with.

The questions — even the fact that you are asking serious questions at all — may be perceived as threatening by the head, pastoral staff or class teachers you speak to. I emphasise that they are intended as a way of opening a dialogue which, with good will, will lead to fruitful co-operation. I hope to explore that co-operation in future books. For now, you may be treading on eggs: how you ask questions is up to you, but do remember that schools are not used to being accountable, or even genuinely informative. Diplomacy will be at a premium.

At the same time, it is advisable to make the checklist you end up with into a group exercise: there is little point in individuals pottering along alone. Make sure that as many parents as possible know of, and discuss, the checklist, and that the school knows that large numbers of people are interested in the answers.

Do give a considerable time for replies, as time is an increasingly rare commodity for harrassed heads. Where possible, have replies given orally, face to face, with summaries on hand-outs. The real answers may be between the lines, with the real dialogue beginning when the supplementary questions follow.

How the dialogue proceeds will be infinitely variable. Some heads and teaching staff will need to overcome much ingrained habit before they can contemplate active co-operation with parents in greening the education of their children. Others, I know, will leap at the chance. I would be interested in practising what we are preaching here by making your process, of reading and acting on this book, a three-dimensional one. This would work in two ways:

1. If you would like to be put in touch with other green parents and teachers, please use *Green Teacher* as a networking contact point. Send a note to this effect, with a £1 coin to cover expenses, and *GT* will twice send you a copy of the list of other people who have done the same. Around the time this book is published, *Green Teacher* will carry a report of this initiative, so that should help to get the ball rolling. The first mailing to you will be a month after you send in; the second will be an update a year later.

2. If you would care to write a piece (no matter that you may not have written before: all the better!) about your experiences in the greening of education — with your children, as parent or as teacher, with your local school or LEA — send it to *GT*. We will then make use of your contribution, in *GT* and/or in a book, to help spread the word and carry on the process.

Good luck!

The checklist

The number after each question is a suggestion as to the person to whom it should be put. **1** = head; **2** = class or subject teacher; **3** = pastoral staff: form tutor, head of year, etc.

1. In what ways do you ensure that each pupil's experience here is a 'Human Scale' experience? **1,3.**

2. Could you see your way to entering 'Flexischooling' arrangements with individual, or groups of, pupils? **1**.

3. In what ways is pupils' work here integrated with the work of the community — excluding schemes aimed at increasing pupils' employability? **1,3**.

4. How many adults, unattached to the education service, are to be found in school at any time, (a) as learners, and (b) as learning resources? **1**.

5. What are the plans for increasing these numbers? **1**.

6. Could I see my child's full, up-to-date records, now, please? **3,1**.

6a. Can my child? **3,1**.

7. How important do you think it is to aim for holistic education? Would you explain, please? **1**.

7a. How do you assess how successful you are being in that aim? **1,2,3**.

8. How do you know whether or not each child is happy here? **1,2,3**.

9. What (and I don't mean RE lessons teaching a religion) help does each pupil receive to enable and encourage the exploration of his/her 'secret heart'? **1,3**.

10. In what ways, with examples (and I don't mean fourth year subject choices) is the curriculum negotiated with pupils? **1**.

11. What inservice training is done now, and planned, specifically to increase staff sensitivity for learning based on exploring pupils' own experiences? **1**.

12. In what ways do you emphasise the importance of building a positive self-image in each pupil? **1,2,3**.

13. How, and how often, is time spent on encouraging the exploration of personal feelings as an integral part of the learning process? **1,2,3**.

14. What are you doing to compensate for the demands of recent legislation, and of industry, for more closed reasoning, narrow analytical, convergent thinking'? **1**.

15. How do you make sure that each pupil knows you are not putting artificial limits on the expectations we, or she/he, have for the pupil? **1**.

16. What are you doing to put more emphasis on process —

learning how to learn, education as a journey of questions — and less on content, getting the right answers? **1,2**.

17. How often in the last two years has a staff meeting openly discussed the full implications of this school's hidden curriculum? Are there plans for (another such) discussion in the foreseeable future? **1**.

18. How would you rate the school, on a scale from 0 to 10, with 0 = dictatorship by the head and management team, and 10 = full, participatory, co-operative democracy? **1,3**.

19. Same as 17, with 'groups of pupils' instead of 'a staff meeting'. **1**.

20. What are you doing to enable and encourage the pupils — now and later — to be active participants in our democracy? **1**.

21. How do you reward responsible disagreement and dissent? **1,2,3**.

22. How are teaching spaces arranged to encourage interaction and exchange, rather than transmission from authority to minions? **3**.

22a. What is the school policy on this? **1**.

23. In what ways are you moving towards 'self-directed learning' for the pupils, with them having responsibility for organising their time? **1,3**.

24. What proportion of a child's work is now done in an integrated, non-compartmentalised way, and what are the plans for increasing the proportion? **1**.

25. How are you increasing the proportion of each child's time which is spent on open-ended investigations, based in reality, away from books? **1,3**.

26. What, specifically, are you doing to ensure equal opportunities for girls, and to encourage girls to assert their rights to take those opportunities? **1,2,3**.

27. What, specifically, are you doing to ensure equal oppor-

tunities for pupils of all ethnic groups, and to encourage them to assert their rights to use those opportunities? **1,2,3**.

28. How do you get round Clause 28, and teach in a civilised way about equal rights for all, regardless of sexual preferences? **1,2,3**.

29. In what ways do you specifically encourage and enable the pupils to learn to co-operate? **1,2**.

30. In what ways is 'education for sustainability' a basic aim of the school? **1**.

31. Which areas of curriculum content are specifically aimed at enabling pupils to think and act ecologically? **1**.

32. In what ways are you greening your subject/class teaching? **1,2**.

33. Could you explain how the school recycling scheme works? **1**.

34. Which environmental agencies and pressure groups are actively involved in assisting learning in the school? **1**.

35. How has your health education programme taken account of recent interest in alternative medicine? **1,3**.

36. Do the meals service and the tuck shop encourage healthy eating? **1.3**.

37. How often have the PR teams of the armed forces been in the school in the last two years? **1**.

37a. Is learning material from the Peace Education Project (or similar) used at or around the time of these visits? **1**.

38. Are representatives of big business allowed into the school to address pupils? In what circumstances? **1**.

38a. Same as 38, substitute 'people from local co-ops'. **1**.

38b. Same as 38, substitute 'local trade unionists'. **1**.

39. Could you give us some of your thoughts on how we, as parents, could get more involved in the life of the school? **1**.

Resources

1. Books on the philosophical background:

Bahro, Rudolf, *Building the Green Movement* (translated by Mary Tyler). Heretic Books, London (1986).

> Any writer who can rise high in East German Communist circles, get himself imprisoned and kicked out, then join the West German Greens, becoming one of their most prominent theorists and activists, then get himself (more or less) kicked out there too, must be worth looking at. This book is a collection of articles and talks that all centre round the long-running dispute in *Die Grünen* on whether, and how far, to compromise with conventional politics. Bahro argues passionately for no compromises, and for concentrating on the spiritual resurgence and the alternative ways of living and working without which the mega-machine will not be undermined.

Bahro, Rudolf, Schumacher Society Lecture 1986. Schumacher Society, Ford House, Hartland, Bideford, Devon.

> A heavy read, and one I have some doubts about, but a powerful polemic, aptly titled 'The logic of deliverance: on the foundations of an ecological politics'.

Capra, Fritjof, *The Turning Point*. Fontana, London (1982).

> If you read only one book that attempts a holistic survey of how our civilisation stands in relation to the mechanistic world view on which it stands, and the new paradigm emerging, read this one.

Dodds, Felix (ed.), *Into the Twenty-first Century*. Green Print, London (1988).

> A collection of views from a variety of sources on the bankruptcy of current politics, and some pointers to the ways ahead: green parliamentary politics?

Porritt, Jonathon, *Seeing Green*. Basil Blackwell, London (1984).

> One of very few green spokespeople with any clout in Britain today, Porritt has the gift of making radical green ideals clear and commonsensical in the eyes of millions of people, via the popular media. This book, an excellent overview, helped establish his position: it is a major source.

Schumacher, E. F., *Small is Beautiful*. Abacus Books, London(1974).

> Of course! Subtitled 'A study of economics as if people mattered', this

227

book, and others of Schumacher, have been among the major influences on the green movement.

Weston, Joe (ed.), *Red and Green*. Pluto Press, London (1986)
If you believe, or have a sneaking suspicion, that some sort of creative fusion will have to come between green politics and a reconstructed socialist politics, try this.

2. Books for building a historical perspective on progressive/radical holistic education

van der Eyken, Willem and Barry Turner, *Adventures in Education*. Penguin, London (1969).
This collection of five pieces, each in its way a story of its own, gives a flavour of the state of excitement and hope around educational innovation in the twenties.

Lawson, John and Harold Silver, *A Social History of Education in England* Methuen, London (1973).
For a detailed, highly readable account of what happened and in what social context, this is the source.

Perry, Leslie R. (ed.), *Russell, Neill, Lane, Kilpatrick. Four progressive educators*. Educational Thinkers Series, Macmillan, London (1967).
Lengthy extracts from their writings: good introduction.

Rusk, Robert R., *Doctrines of the great educators*. Macmillan, London(1969).
This has been a major source for education students for a very longtime: the 1969 edition is the fourth, after many reprints of all the previous three.

Simon, Brian (ed.), *The Radical Tradition in Education in Britain*. Lawrenceand Wishart, London (1972).
A valuable source for placing in context many educational arguments current today and tomorrow.

3. Books to help with rethinking education today

Bruner, Jerome, *The Process of Education*. Harvard University Press, Harvard (1960).
Rather academic for most people's needs, but a crucial work in the discussion on education as process, not product.

Freire, Paulo, *Pedagogy of the Oppressed* (translated by Myra Bergman-Ramos). Penguin, London (1972).
  Freire worked with illiterate peasants in Brazil, and developed critiques of education in the context of the dominant culture that are relevant all round the world.

Goodman, Paul, *Growing up Absurd*. Victor Gollancz, London (1961). *Compulsory Miseducation*. Penguin, London (1971).
  One of the saddest things about education today is how relevant these two books still are, almost thirty years after they were written, on the wastage and destruction of people involved in education for the mega-machine.

Green Party Education Working Group, *Routes to Change*. Green Party, London (1988).
  A collection of essays, of very variable quality indeed, but a useful picture of the state of play in that particular group. Check with party HQ for the latest document.

Holt, John, *How children Fail*. Penguin, London (1969).
  For many people, the seminal work on the shortcomings of our approach to education-in-school.

Holt, John, *Instead of Education*. Penguin, London (1976).
  Opening up the whole discussion of how, and where, education can best be done.

Lacey, Colin, and Ray Williams, (eds), *Education, Ecology and Development*, WWF and Kogan Page, London (1987).
  A collection of seminar papers, some of whose authors are in *Red and Green*, making the case collectively for an education network of people concerned with the relationship between human and natural systems.

Meighan, Roland, *Flexischooling*. Education Now Books, PO Box 186,Ticknall, Derbyshire DE7 1WF.
  Roland Meighan, a Senior Lecturer in Education at Birmingham, has been studying and writing about new developments at the sharp end of innovation for a long time. This book is a clear, simple and concise outline of the excellent case for flexischooling.

Meighan and Harber (eds.); *The Democratic School*, Education New Books, Ticknall (1989).
  An excellent collection, from some of the best people in the field, on the democratisation of education.

Nicholson, Brian, *Freedom, Knowledge and Education*. Ninth Curry Lecture, University of Exeter (1986).
  Nicholson was the last head of Dartington school, and this lecture is a celebration of the best of the Dartington tradition, and a compelling discussion of a possible future.

Rogers, Carl, *On becoming a person*. Constable (1967).
Freedom to Learn for the 80's. Merrill (1983).

Rogers' are the leading works in the application of humanistic psychology to education. Readable and punchy.

Shor, Ira, *Culture Wars: Schools and Society in the Conservative Restoration, 1969–1984*. Routledge & Kegan Paul, London (1986).
What happened to all the hopes and dreams, the hard work and the changed consciousnesses, of the 1960s in education? This important book traces the decline brought about by the right wing backlash in the USA: it rings very many bells for British readers too.

Social Alternatives, Vol. 4. No. 2, July (1984).
This is an excellent journal produced by members of the Department of External Studies, University of Queensland. This issue, 'Radicalising Schooling', is superb in itself and in giving us Brits an Oz perspective.

Toogood, Philip, *Minischooling*. Human Scale Education Movement.
Please buy this for any large-school headteacher you know who has a mind open enough to consider learning some lessons from it. Much of the detail may not be transferrable, but as at least a beginning of the answer to the problem of size, it is wonderful.

Whitaker, Patrick, *Education as if People Mattered*. Occasional paper No.3, Centre for Peace Studies, St Martin's College, Lancaster.
A short, dense but readable account of how radical, deeply green ideals can be applied, to an extent, today. Should be required reading for all teachers. The author is an adviser in Derbyshire.

4. Books on curriculum changes

Braham, Mark, The Ecology of Education. In *New Ideas in Environmental Education* (ed. Briceno & Pitt). Croom Helm/IUCN, London (1988).
Mark Braham works at the Centre for Integrative Education in Geneva, and not surprisingly, therefore, produces a stimulating essay. The rest of the book is patchy but useful.

Early Years Education Project, *Educating the Whole Child*. University of London Institute of Education (1989).
A video and book package introducing the holistic approach; supported by curriculum materials. I have not seen these: they are just coming out as I write, but they sound excellent.

Fisher, Simon and David Hicks, *World Studies 8–13, a Teacher's Handbook*. Oliver & Boyd, Edinburgh (1985).
Similar in many ways to *Global Teacher*, but worth a look in its own right.

Greig, Sue, Graham Pike, and David Selby, *Earthrights*. Kogan Page & World Wildlife Fund, London (1987).

The Centre for Global Education at York, who ran the Global Impact project of which this book is a part, is one of the most, if not *the* most, vital curriculum development projects in Britain today. Their work with teachers, schools and materials, on future-oriented, activity-based education with a global perspective is very influential and should be more so. If your school doesn't have a copy of this book, it should have, and if your LEA has not yet arranged to talk to the people at York, then it should.

Hicks, David (ed.), *Education for Peace*. Routledge, London (1988).

A superb collection of pieces from across the range of curricular areas and real-world issues with which peace education concerns itself. Set in context, with a major case study on each, and good supporting material on the way forward for change.

Mares, Cherry and Robert Stephenson, *Inside, Outside*. The Tidy Britain Group schools research project, Brighton Polytechnic.

Masheder, Mildred, *Let's Co-operate*. Peace Education Project, Peace Pledge Union, 6 Endsleigh Street, London WC1 (1986).

A wonderful compilation of activities for younger children for peaceful conflict-solving via positive self-image, creativity, communication, etc.

Nicholas, Frances, *Coping with Conflict*. Learning Development Aids Project, Duke Street, Wisbech, Cambridgeshire, PE13 2AE.

Useful material for use with the 8 to 12 age group.

Parry, Mike, 'Planning and implementing environmental curriculum initiatives in . . . schools. . .'. National Association for Environmental Education, Occasional Paper No. 11 (1987).

Rather detailed and academic for most usual purposes, but if you or your local school are getting serious about environmental work, this booklet should be at hand.

Pike, Graham, and David Selby, *Global Teacher, Global Learner*. Hodder and Stoughton, London (1988).

From the Centre for Global Education in York, this is *the* practical manual. If any reader is saying 'Yes, I do want to go into active learning for a future of ecological sustainability and human peace and justice', that reader needs this book.

Robottom, Ian (ed.), *Environmental Education: Practice and Possibility*. Deakin University, Victoria, 3217, Australia.

A fascinating view of how radical Australian educators have been thinking around the question 'What is environmental education all about, and why?' See especially Noel Gough's piece, 'Learning with Environments, an Ecological Paradigm for Education', which appeared in *Green Teacher* 8.

Slaughter, Richard, *The Futures Kit*. Department of Educational Research, Lancaster University, Lancaster LA1 4YL (1987).

A folder containing several excellent background papers for the teacher, and the book *Futures: Tools and Techniques*, which is all you need to get going in the classroom.

Toft, Peter, *CDT for GCSE*, Heinemann Educational Books, London.
Provides an excellent guide for students on how to design for people.

5. Periodicals

AREE, the Annual Review of Environmental Education, edited by Steven Sterling, published by the Council for Environmental Education (address in organisations).

Educare, published by the Universal Education Association.
Now defunct, ran 1984–85. Worth seeking out back copies in a good education library.

Education Now, PO Box 186, Ticknall, Derbys, DE7 1WF.
Arose out of Human Scale Education Movement. Deep and broad. Edited by Philip Toogood.

Green Education Newsletter; newsletter of the Green Party Education Policy Working Group. Jonathan Sherlock, 183 Brooks Lane, Whitwick, Leicestershire, LE6 4DZ.
Extremely patchy in quality, but worth a look for keeping abreast of developments.

Green Teacher, Machynlleth, Powys, SY20 8DN. Six issues per year. Send SAE for information on availability of back issues. Photocopies of out of print issues: £3.60 + postage.

Holistic Education Review, PO Box 1476, Greenfield, MA 01302, USA.
More words, more concentrated focus, but with different theme each time. Edited by Ron Miller. Excellent publication.

Insight, series from Christian Aid Education Department, PO Box 100, London, SE1 7RT.
Regular high-quality curriculum material.

Lib Ed, The Cottage, The Green, Leire, Leics, LE17 5HL.
'A magazine for the liberation of learning'; anarchist.

Lifelines, Education Department, Worldwide Fund for Nature, Panda House, Weyside Park, Godalming, Surrey, GU7 1XR.
Education as if the earth really mattered. The newsletter of the education dept of the WWF. Goes free to every school. Well done. Worth digging out if you haven't seen it yet.

New Internationalist, 42 Hythe Bridge Street, Oxford, OX1 2EP.
Number 180, February 1988 'Wisdom and Wealth, the Great Education Hoax' was an outstanding issue.

Resurgence, Ford House, Hartland, Bideford, Devon.

For many people, *the* magazine to read for inspiration and information for whole-person nourishment. Recent issues on education: No. 130, Sept.–Oct. '88, and No. 118, Sep.–Oct. '86.

Skipping Stones, 80574 Hazelton Road, Cottage Grove, OR97424, USA.

A multi-ethnic children's forum. All contributions by children, around the theme of the 'stewardship of the ecological web that sustains us', encouraging co-operation and creativity. My eleven year old loved issue 1, January 1989. So did I.

Unite! UNA Youth, UNA Youth Council, 3 Whitehall Court, London, SW1A 2EL.

An internationalist magazine by young people for young people.

6. Organisations

Bridge Educational Trust. Address: enquire via *Green Teacher*.

Promotes holistic education by sponsoring publications, networking and bringing together people and organisations working in parallel ways.

Centre for Alternative Technology, Machynlleth, Powys, SY20 9AZ.

Europe's only such visitor centre dealing with renewable energy, conservation, organic growing, ecology, and working towards holism. Receives groups of pupils and students on day visits and on made-to-measure residential courses. Publishes curriculum material.

Centre for Global Education, York University, Heslington, York, YO1 5DD.

Centre for Peace Studies, St Martin's College, Lancaster, LA1 3JD.

Has run the World Studies 8–13 project, holds courses and conferences, and publishes, on peace education.

Centre for World Development Education, Regent's College, Inner Circle, Regent's Park, London, NW1 4NS.

Publishes and promotes a wide range of development education material.

The Circle Dance Network can be contacted through *The Grapevine* (their journal) at 17 Vernon Road, Chester, Cheshire, CH1 4JT.

Conservation Trust, George Palmer Site, Northumberland Ave., Reading, Berks, RG2 7PW.

Produces and catalogues large amounts of material for environmental education.

Council for Environmental Education. School of Education, London Rd, Reading, RG1 5AQ.

The clearing house for information on all aspects of environmental education; produces resource lists and regular newsletter.

Earth Education: for details of workshops, contact Graham McDonald, Ballater Field Study Centre, Aberdeen, AB3 5RJ.

Education for Neighbourhood Change, School of Education, University of Nottingham, NG7 2RD.

Promotes active participation by children in developing their neighbourhood. Produces materials, project ideas, and information on ongoing projects.

Education Otherwise, 25 Common Lane, Hemingford Abotts, Cambs. PE18 9AN, *and* Children's Home-Based Education Association, 14 Basel Ave., Armthorpe, Doncaster, Yorks.

Two information and support services for parents thinking of, or doing, home schooling.

Friends of the Earth, 26–28 Underwood St, London N1 7JQ.

Produce large amounts of material useful in various ways in schools, and have an education worker.

Green College, Pickersleigh Court, Malvern, Worcs, WR1 2ET. Tel. 0865–249020, London office 01–674–0763.

Human Scale Education Movement, c/o Dame Catherine's School, Ticknall, Derbyshire.

Campaigns and publishes.

Intermediate Technology Development Group, Myson House, Railway Terrace, Rugby, CV21 3HT.

Has a thriving education section, which answers enquiries and produces good material.

Islington Schools Environment Project, c/o Robert Blair School, Blundell St., London, N7 9BL.

'Playstructures' is available from CSV Advisory Service, 237 Pentonville Rd, London N1 9NJ, price £3.50 + 50p p&p. Highly recommended!

Lifelab, 1156 High St., Santa Cruz, CA., 95064, USA.

Produce the set of three books of curriculum on 'learning by growing': one of the best curriculum projects I have ever come across. For the three books, send $35 plus $3 surface mail or $15 air mail for UK orders.

NADEC (National Association of Development Education Centres), 6 Endsleigh St., London, WC1.

Provides information and co-ordination service for the local centres, each of which is independent. Ask them where your nearby centres are.

National Association of City Farms, Old Vicarage, 66 Fraser St., Windmill Hill, Bedminster, Bristol, BS3 4LY.

National Association for Environmental Education, West Midlands College of HE, Gorway, Walsall, WS1 3BD.

Publishes valuable newsletter and occasional papers.

Nature Conservancy Council, Northminster House, Peterborough, PE1 1UA.
   Has an active education department, which publishes good material.

New Education Directory, tel. 0272 735091. An excellent new information sevice about alternative education in Britain, run by Poppy Green.

New University, 24 South Rd., Hockley, Birmingham, B18 5NB.

Oaktree Education Trust, 24 Aigburth Drive, Sefton Park, Liverpool, L17 4JH.
   Send £1 for brochure containing the story of Oaktree School. Inspiring!

Peace Education Project, Peace Pledge Union, 6 Endsleigh St., London, WC1.
   Produce regular newsletter and curricular material.

Play for Life. For details write to Play for Life, 31B Ipswich Road, Norwich, NR2 2LN, UK.

Scottish Environmental Education Council, c/o Biology Dept, Paisley College, High St., Paisley, PA1 2BE.

Tidy Britain Group Schools Research Project, Polytechnic, Brighton, BN2 2JY.
   Publish a wide range of high quality material to assist with active environmental education.

The Trust for Urban Ecology. For information on Trust activities plus a publications list, write to: The Secretary, Trust for Urban Ecology, Old Loom House, Backchurch Lane, London, E1.

Urban Spaces Scheme, Polytechnic of North London, Holloway Rd., London, N7 8DB.
   Produce a very wide range of materials for urban ecology work.

Worldwide Fund for Nature, Panda House, Weybridge Park, Godalming, Surrey, GU7 1XR.
   Very large range of excellent materials, particularly the 'Global Environmental Education Project'.

7. Working the system: sources of assistance

Publications

Carter, Trevor and Jean Coussins, *Shattering Illusions*. Lawrence & Wishart, London (1987).
   Well-respected account of the struggle to get racial equality taken seriously.

Education Rights Handbook. Children's Legal Centre, London (1987).

Glatter, Ron (ed.), *Understanding School Management*, Open University Press, Milton Keynes (1988).

Local Management of Schools. Free DES leaflet.

Mortimer, Peter *et al.*, *School Matters: The Junior Years*. Open Books, London (1988).

Report of a large research project in ILEA; discusses the factors that make some schools more successful, and outlines the difficulties in making comparisons.

Taylor, Felicity, *Parents' Rights in Education*. Longman, London (1986).

A very readable guide.

Organisations

Children's Legal Centre, 20 Compton Terrace, London, N1 2UN.

Commission for Racial Equality, Eliot House, 10 Allington Street, London, SW1E 5EH.

Equal Opportunities Commission, Overseas House, Quay Street, Manchester, M3 3HN.

Department of Education and Science, Elizabeth House, 39 York Road, London, SE1 7PH.

National Association of School Governors and Managers, 10 Brookfield Park, London, NW5 1ER.